Letters from North Africa

1943 - 1944

Letters from North Africa
1943 -1944
This map is just intended to show locations of bases where I served during this period.

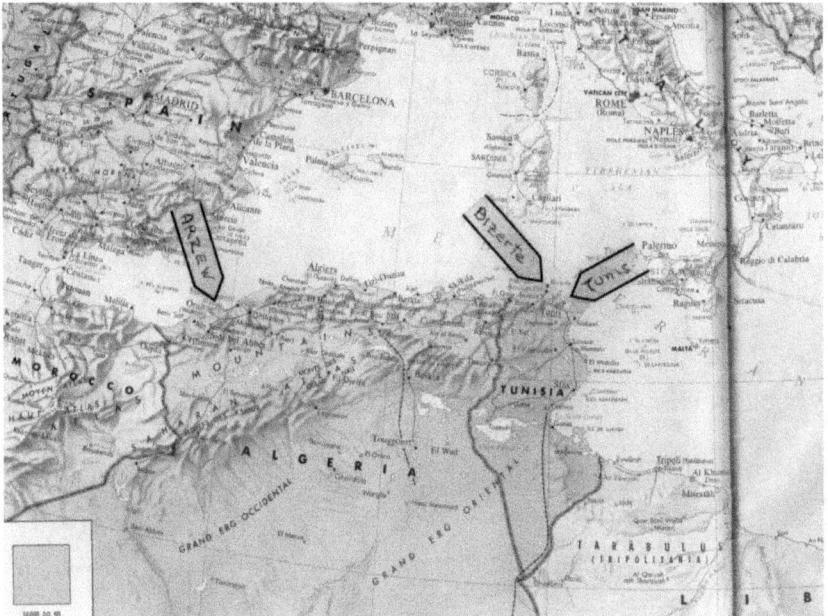

By Arnleif Jensen
with enormous help from
wife Marie S. Jensen
who painstakingly
transcribed the hand written
letters and designed
the back cover,
plus editing many times

Letters from North Africa
1943 - 1944

Published by ArnMar Press
Seneca, SC
arnmarpr@gmail.com

Other books by the author:

A SON OF NORWAY, HIS MEMORIES 1919 - 1946

A SON OF NORWAY, HIS MEMORIES Volume 2 1946 -1980

ISBN: 978-0-9720807-3-6

Printed in

The United States of America

Dedicated to all American
service people,
Army and its Air Corps,
Navy, Marines, Coast Guard,
and
Merchant Marine sailors,
who served overseas in
World War II.

Introduction

When the Coast Guard troop ship USS Samuel Chase sailed from Bayonne, NJ, in early March of 1943, it carried me (newly minted Ensign Jensen) and 1500 other Navy personnel to set up bases in North Africa in support of the coming Sicilian and Anzio invasions. We did not know we were heading for Africa. When our ship landed in Oran, Algeria, in late March, we found out where we were. Rommel and his Afrika Korps were still fighting the British army and allies in Egypt and Libya.

From Oran a large contingent of men, along with many trucks and supplies, was sent east to Arzew (see map), a resort town that had been evacuated by the local inhabitants. There we set up a temporary base, awaiting the complete withdrawal of the Germans from North Africa. When that was completed in mid-May of 1943, AATB YOKE (code name for Arzew) was essentially disbanded and moved by LST (Landing Ship Tank) to Bizerte, Tunisia. AATB stands for "Advanced Amphibious Training Base", and was used as a partial cover for a number of activities, including some training in amphibious techniques. As the name implies, LSTs were designed to carry tanks and large armored vehicles. The novel feature of these ships was that the bow was built so that it could open wide when the ship was driven onto a beach, for unloading of the tanks.

I was in Bizerte for less than a week. During that time the Germans were angry at being evicted from Africa and showed that anger by sending bombers over the naval base where we were billeted for a couple of nights. Their bombardiers had lousy aim, and most of the bombs exploded harmlessly in nearby empty fields. I still remember the ack-ack anti-aircraft guns firing at the bombers - what a sight, it lit up the sky! That was the only time I came under harm's way during my active duty service. Soon I received orders to "Report to Commanding Officer, AATB X-ray", code name for Tunis and LaGoulette, a suburb of Tunis. I hope this makes the following letters a little more meaningful.

Today, we are familiar with the idea of our servicemen overseas communicating face-to-face with their loved ones at home via Skype, but during World War II, there was no Internet, no e-mail, no cell phones or other means of fast communication for service people stationed overseas. Therefore regular postal mail and newly developed V-Mail were the only methods by which communication was available to them. V-Mail was a system in which the writer wrote his letter on a special one-page form, which was photographed. The film, containing many such letters, was sent Stateside by plane, where it was developed and the letters were printed and mailed to the recipients. It worked in both directions, and was supposed to be much faster than regular mail, which took from two weeks to well over a month. V-Mail ideally took about eight days for a letter to arrive, and had the added benefit of a comparatively small volume of weight/space taken on the planes.

This collection of all the letters I sent home during the two years I was in North Africa remained intact because my dear mother saved every one. When both mother and father were gone and only sister Violet remained in the family flat on 70th Street in Brooklyn, she was the custodian. When she died in 1986, my brother Aleck found them when cleaning out the premises. He sent the letters to me. When I showed them to Marie, she immediately said, "They would make a great historical book for those interested in WWII service accounts". That was several years ago and the idea was put aside in favor of higher priority work.

All military personnel sent out of the continental United States were under strict orders not to say anything in letters home about 'present detailed location', base personnel manning, duty details and other no-no's under pain of razor excision by the censor officers. That was the reason we could only write on one side of the sheet. As one of my duties as an officer was censoring enlisted men's letters, there were a few times that I had to use the razor and leave holes in a man's letter, but private mentioning to the offender and others who pushed the line soon reduced the frequency of this.

Cast of characters: Norwegian immigrants Mom, a housewife, and Dad, captain of an oil tanker plying the waters of

8

New York harbor, Long Island Sound and the Hudson River, brother Aleck, a private in the Army attempting pilot training, and sister Violet, age 15. Other correspondents referenced include University sweetheart Virginia, University roommate Loren, another University girlfriend Jean Anne, and Roy Lindberg, a long time 'best friend'.

Note: Many insertions have been made 70 years later to add information I could not write in the letters, plus pictures that help illustrate some passages. The inserted text is shown in *Italics*. I have also chosen to add several episodes that I really didn't want to write about to the family. As you read them you will know why.

Before I received the order to board the Coast Guard ship, I had gone to Manhattan to a large photographic shop and bought a camera and film that I thought would be fun to have wherever I was sent. This was a high grade camera called "Super Iconta B" with a Schneider f/2.8 lens and Compur shutter with speeds of 1/500 second in steps to 1/10 second and then 'timed' exposure. It took 120 and 620 size films but instead of full frame pictures, eight to a roll, my camera took half frame pictures giving me sixteen pictures per roll. This camera, with five rolls of film, was packed in my gear. Only later did I find out cameras were not supposed to be part of my outfit. Too late! And so it turned out that I was the only one on my first three bases who had a camera, and this later resulted in my being named "Official Base Photographer".

I recently discovered in storage a small collection of mimeographed "newssheets" that were distributed to our base personnel, keeping us informed about the progress of the war. I have included a few excerpts from these, where it seemed appropriate. They are in SMALL CAPS, to differentiate them from other text.

Note. Some readers may note the difference in the spelling of my name in the copyright page and author's name. Arnleiv is my American legal name, applied at Ellis Island in 1927. Arnleif is my Norwegian baptismal name, given to me April 13, 1919.

Here I also want to express my deep appreciation to retired Clemson University professor, Dr. John Wagner, for his extensive and detailed edit read of this book's final proof copy.

Letter from North Africa
1943

Somewhere in North Africa
(Arzew Resort, Algeria N.A.)
March 23, 1943

Dear Mom & Dad,

We have finally arrived at our destination – safe and sound. We had a good trip across – no trouble at all. There isn't much I can tell you about the trip or of the place we are at now. While on the ship, I stood some watches – hold watch, stern lookout, and bridge lookout. It was good experience and I kinda enjoyed it.

I met our chaplain when we started out – a really fine fellow by the name of Silseth – we call him "Padre" or Mike. He is from Minneapolis – went to school at Northwestern Seminary out there. He and I are good friends now – we visited Oran together. It is an interesting town. Believe it or not, I have already picked up a few words of French, and I expect to learn more as time goes by.

Thanks so much for forwarding Virginia's letter – it really means a lot to get mail. I am going to try to get permission for you to send me a package – there are a few things I can use very well which are impossible to obtain here. But just wait on that till you hear from me again.

I didn't have time to pick up my pay account before leaving, so I won't be paid for about a month. However, I have enough money to last until then so don't worry about that. The only thing that bothers me is that I won't be able to send you any money for perhaps a month and a half or two. I hope it won't inconvenience you to take care of my bill at Macy's *(uniform shop)* and perhaps my Lutheran Brotherhood insurance until I can start sending some money. When I can get it arranged, I shall send $100 a month home. Of that, $50 is for you, to repay my school debt – the rest to pay what bills I owe, and if any is left, would you start a bank account for me? I intend to save as much money as possible so that I will have something when I come back.

You will notice that I am writing on one side of the paper only. That is for censoring purposes. If anything has been cut out of this letter, you will know I said something I shouldn't have. Incidentally, I will get my mail much quicker if you send it air-mail. And would you forward any mail I may get as soon as possible?

I miss you all very much – and we are all going to try and get this war won quickly so that we can go back home soon. Give my regards to Aleck, and a kiss to Violet.

Good night and much love to you all,

Arne

Ens. Arnleiv Jensen

P.S. Please don't worry – as everything is fine.

AATB ARZEW
ALGERIA,
First Duty Station
on the
Dark Continent!

This is the title slide for a slide show I have made of my time in North Africa.

This was called Tent City and provided quarters for the enlisted men.

Postcard, postmarked March, 29, 1943.

Dear Mother & Dad,

Everything fine. Had a talk by the Captain this morning. He suggested you not writing until you hear from me – about a month.

I'm sorry I missed you before leaving, Dad, but guess it couldn't be helped.

Regards and love to Violet.

Love,
Arne

Dear Folks,

I imagine you are still waiting to hear from me – but if I remember correctly, there should be one or two letters arriving for you soon. We are being kept busy all the time so there isn't very much time to write – and there isn't a great deal I can tell you either. *(I tried to think about what 'being busy' included, but 70 years later nothing specific came to mind.)* We are living in a cottage on the seashore, and although it isn't completely furnished yet, in time it will be very comfortable and cozy. I think I told you our convoy came across safely - without a bit of trouble.

Former resort building called Hotel Gazelle

Since we have been here, we have had a number of air raid alerts, but no planes have approached closer than 100 miles or so. All in all, it seems to be a comparatively safe place to be at.

Up to now, I haven't been doing any engineering work, but have received notice that I am to start that within a day or two. In the meantime, I have been on various work details, and have stood Officer-of-the-Guard watches. These duties have been interesting, but I'll be glad when I start work in my own line here.

You should see how tanned my face is – you'd hardly recognize me. And we get excellent food – as good as or better than the average people get back home. I don't think I'm gaining much weight, but I'm getting harder and healthier by the hour. --- This is the only place I've ever seen where there can be mud and dust at the same time. We have had some rain lately – and everything turned to mud. But it isn't so bad, for we have clothes to use for the particular weather at hand.

It is chow time – so that's all for now.

Loads and loads of love to all of you.

Arne

These officers' quarters in resort cottages were certainly more comfortable than the "tent city" where the enlisted personnel lived.

North Africa
March 31, 1943

Dear Mom & Dad,

Another day is done, and I have a few minutes in which to write a few letters. Last night I wrote one by candlelight because the electric lights were out of commission, but tonight they are on again.

Have I told you we are living in a cottage on the sea? There are a group of them which at one time must have been a summer resort. It's a nice place, with plastered walls and cement floor. There are two double-decker bunks in each room. The house isn't completely furnished yet, but it will be in a short time. The Navy has issued us blankets, sheets & pillow cases & towels –

Officers on laundry detail

so everything is pretty well taken care of. Our laundry facilities are not set up yet, so I have done some washing myself – but there are some dirty shirts and pants which I won't tackle for I haven't any iron. Today I hung out my bedding and aired it in the sun – it's going to be nice to crawl in the bunk tonight. Also heated some water today, and took a "bucket" bath – that is, I washed myself out of a pail. It's the first chance I've had for a long time and it sure felt great.

Haven't had any mail outside of Virginia's letter yet, but imagine there must be some on the way. It was foolish to advise you not to write until you heard from me – for I understand there are mail planes going across every day – and in that case, I would probably have had lots of letters by now. It's hard to put into words just how much mail means to the boys away from home – but take it from me, it means a lot. This must be all for now. My love to Violet – and to the two best parents in the world.

Arne

16

P.S. Please don't worry about me, for I am just about as safe here as I would be in New York. How is Aleck getting along? Would you send me his address – I'll try and drop him a line. Regards to all my friends – and greet Pastor Okdale for me. Let me know how much longer it takes for this letter to go than the air mail letters I've sent.

V-Mail form
For the reader not familiar with V-mail, a short description follows. This form is standard letter size, with headers to fill in. When the letter is written and ready for sending, it is folded and given to the local post office. It is then sent to a base where it is microfilmed with hundreds of others, then flown to the U.S. where it is developed, enlarged and printed on paper, and then mailed, folded so contents are not visible other than addressee. The reverse is true for V-mail originating in the U.S. I will try to reproduce a few of the clearer ones later on. On the following page is a transcription of one of many.

V-Mail Form
From Ens. A Jensen, USNR
Navy 232 c/o Fleet Post Office – New York, N.Y.
(This was for Arzew)
April 13, 1943

Dear Mom & Dad,

Congratulations on your twenty-fifth anniversary. I really wish I could have been home for the great occasion, but then things just didn't work out that way. I had planned on buying you a nice present, but that also was made impossible. As soon as I get paid, I shall send you some money which is to be used for buying yourselves a present – and for nothing else!

Today I had a letter from you dated March 4th, and a few days ago (three to be exact) I had one dated the 20th from Virginia – so you can see what the mail situation is like. Keep writing as often as you can.

We have been very busy lately. I get up in the morning at 6:15 and I'm not through until 10:30 or 11:00 at night. It is now after eleven and I am plenty tired. It is a problem for me now to find time to wash out my socks and things like that---but I'll manage somehow.

I got a letter from the Navy today and now I can finally arrange to have some money sent to you regularly as we had planned, but it might not start coming until late June or first part of July.

Too bad I missed your anniversary, but I'll be there to help you celebrate your fiftieth and golden anniversary.

All my love,

Arne

V-mail form
From Ens. A Jensen, USNR
Navy 232
c/o Fleet Post Office NY
April 15, 1943

Dear Mom & Dad,

   I was happy today – I received four letters from you, and the "Sentinel" *(church newsletter)* from Bethany. You can't imagine how much it means to get mail regularly here – most everybody seems to live for that moment in the afternoon when the mail arrives.

   This check of mine you wrote about --- it can't be my pay check, for I get paid over here. Perhaps it was the $100 uniform allowance. In any case, see if you can deposit it in my name in the bank – but also see if you can't arrange to draw on it so that you can pay whatever bills I owe. And please Mom, keep a record of all you pay out for me out of your own pocket so that I can repay you. When you pay my insurance, don't pay for double indemnity and waiver of premium any more. The company was going to write about that. Did they?

   I am sorry to hear you had a cold, Mom --- hope you are all over it now. I had a little cold, too, for awhile, but it is all gone now. The dust bothered my throat, but in time you get used to it.

   It was nice to hear you had a letter from Virginia --- you should have some letters from me also by this time. I heard tonight that V-mail service has been set up for us at last, so if you send your mail that way, I should get it about 8 days later. And write often, every other day if you can.

   I'm certainly glad to hear Aleck is doing so well with his flying --- and George and Jack too. Keep me posted on how they are.

   Everything is fine with me --- and who knows, I might be back sooner than you think. Take care of yourselves.

Love,
Arne

Ens. A. Jensen

V-mail form

From Ens. A. Jensen, USNR
Navy 232, c/o Fleet Post Office
New York, N.Y.
April 17, 1943
 Dear Mom & Dad,
        The day after I received your letter dated March 4th, I got
your other one dated March 29th – isn't that funny? However, I
was happy to get them – doesn't make any difference when they
were mailed – as long as they come.
        Today is Palm Sunday, and this afternoon we had church
services and communion. It was very impressive, even in the
simplicity of a tent chapel. I enjoyed it very much. Did I tell you
that the chaplain is a very good friend of
mine – and comes from Minneapolis?
Before all this work came up, we were
together quite often, but as a rule, it's only at
chow time I meet him now. Outside of the
fact that we had a couple of hours off for
church today, it was just like any other day.
Maybe next year it will be different –
anyway, we will hope and pray that it will.

Chaplain Mike Sislith

        Next Sunday (Easter) we are having a sunrise service –
which I am looking forward to very much. I have been to quite a
few Easter sunrise services, but
this one should be quite
different. It will mean more to
us out here, you can be sure.
Space grows short so I must
close with a wish for a blessed
Easter for you all at home.
Greet Pastor Okdale and his
family for me too.

                All my love,
                Arne

Easter sunrise service

North Africa
April 24, 1943
Dear Mom, Dad, & Violet –

Here it is almost Easter, and I am almost unaware of it. Last night they had Good Friday services, but I had to miss it

Chapel tent service

because I was on duty. Tomorrow morning we are having sunrise service at 6:00 AM – and I'll be there, for I may not get to the regular church hour. I've been granted permission to take pictures of it, so I'll have something to show you when I get back.

(The picture in the previous letter is really from that sunrise service.)

A few days ago was payday – and I am enclosing two money orders – one for $100 which you will take care of the way we planned (fifty in the bank for me, and fifty as part repayment of what I owe you). The one for $25 is my present to you for your 25th anniversary. It is to be used in buying yourselves an appropriate present, perhaps that silver set you wanted, Mom. Under no circumstances are you to use it for anything else, O.K.?

Me with Med in background

I would have written before this, but have been working all day and evenings too – and when I get back to my room, all I want to do is flop in the sack and lay there until morning. Pretty soon there won't be work every evening, and then I'll have a chance to write more often.

You should see me now - I'm in the best of health, have a swell suntan on my face contrasting with my light hair, which is

21

now much lighter than when you saw me last. And my eyebrows are bleached white too. I've gained six or seven pounds since leaving the States and eating like a horse. I'm even growing a mustachio on my upper lip - makes me look a little older.

Must close now, and go on duty. Please don't worry about me because this is about as safe as N.Y. is, if not safer.

All my love and affection to the best family I know.

Your son,
Arne

P.S. You are allowed to send me packages (no more than 5 lbs, 15 inches long and 36 inches in length and girth combined). Please send me some air mail writing paper (with Navy insignia if possible), that brown flashlight in the drawer & batteries (2) for it, a string or chain for my dog tag, a pocket knife, and if you are allowed to (ask Post Office) as much film for my camera as possible, size 120 (Kodak SuperXX or PanatomicX), or size B2 (Agfa Ansco Superpan Supreme). Thanks a million, and take it out of my money.

I will add some pictures from Arzew on this open page.

Mediterranean Sea

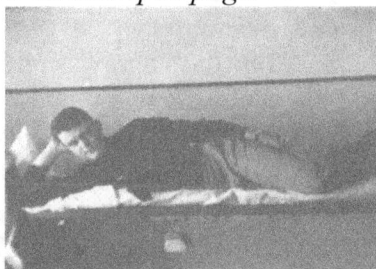

Ens. Penner, my roommate, on bunk above mine (230 lb.)

Officers on censor duty

V-mail form

From: Ens. A Jensen, USNR
Navy 232, c/o Fleet P.O.
New York, N.Y.
April 30, 1943
Dear Mom, Dad, & Violet,

I'm sorry I haven't had a chance to write sooner – it's the same old story – busy from morning to night. As usual, there isn't a great deal to say, but I am feeling fine – have put on about eight pounds since I left New York. You should see the tan I have – think I told you about that. Where I am now, the food is excellent – bet I'm eating better than you folks back home. However, our laundry situation isn't quite set up yet, so I have been washing out some of my own, and sending the rest out to local French families. They charge just as much as the laundries back home do.

    I had a letter from Aleck a few days ago – it was really swell to hear from him. I know he won't be able to write very often, so you keep me informed of his progress. I also had a letter from Loren and Virginia yesterday, but believe me, it was really a pleasure. Your last letters are over a week old now – hope I hear from you again soon.

    Easter has come and gone and I hope you had an enjoyable season. Mother's Day is coming up very soon – and although I won't be home to help celebrate the occasion, I want to wish you the best of everything, Mother, and don't you worry about me. I am all right, and we'll all be back together again someday.

All my love,
Arne

May 8, 1943

Dear Mother,

I was a very happy fellow yesterday --- I got seven letters all at once. One of them from you was from Mar. 12, another April 7, and one each from you and Dad dated April 14. Then I got one from Loren dated the 14th of April, and one from Virginia from March 29th, and the letter from the Electrical Engineering Society. I was very glad to know that you have started receiving my letters – no doubt you were worrying some before they came. Have you received the letter with my first money orders in it yet? I am enclosing another order for $100 in this letter to be used according to our plan. Hope to have some money saved up for myself when I return to the states.

I am now on the Admiral's staff – can't say what I'm doing but it's very interesting --- and it might lead to some good opportunities. I had to move a distance to new quarters which aren't as good as the ones I had, but the food here is much better – excellent compared to what we had at the other place.

I had my laundry done the other day – by local French girls – was quite expensive, and not done as well as I would expect. Cost me $3.06 for three shirts, three khaki pants, khaki coat (one), 3 sets of underwear (shorts & shirts), 5 pr. socks, 4 handkerchiefs, and a light wind-breaker, and one towel. If I had the time and iron, I'd do it all myself. It is certain anyway, that no one has ever done my laundry as well as you used to do it.

It's funny that you got my letter of Mar. 30 or 31st first because I wrote one or two before that – as soon as we arrived here – that was about Mar. 21 or 22. But then the mails are not very reliable to Africa and you should get them in time. Did you get the letter requesting a package? If you haven't already sent it, would you include 2 or three black ties, please?

I miss you a lot Mom, but things are looking up and maybe in the near future (I hope) we'll be home again. Regards to all the family and relatives & friends.

Love and kisses,

Arne

The assignment to the Admiral's chateau was, in essence, an engineering posting, since I was an electrical engineer. That is stretching it a bit, because my duty there was to become a Communications Officer. I had three weeks of intensive training in codes and ciphers, especially the ECM — Electric Ciphering Machine.

On this machine, one typed in a plain-text message, and, after the machine did its thing, out came a paper tape containing 5-letter coded groups that were pasted on a standard letter paper, with a date/time and header info added. Now it was ready for wireless radio transmission. The receiving party typed these groups into his machine, with the same settings given in the header, and out came the original plain text message.

I was to spend the rest of my active duty time as a Communications Officer.

Northwest Africa
May 10, 1943

Dear Dad,

It was so nice to get your letter – it made me feel very good. The last few days I've really hit the jackpot as far as mail is concerned. Day before yesterday I got seven letters, yesterday one letter, and today nine letters. Of those 17, ten were from you and Mother. It is really swell to get letters – makes a fellow feel sure the home folks are thinking about him.

My present job is very interesting – and the best part of it all is that it keeps me busy most of the time. I do have some time for myself now – which I didn't have before. I am learning a lot of things which might be very valuable to me in later life.

How is everything with you? From one of Mother's letters, she intimated that there was something going on at the Union. Sure hope there won't be any trouble – but hope you get a raise too. Greet Andy and the other men I know – Tom, the cook, and John, the watchman, and all the others.

I think I would rather be on a ship than having a shore job – but chances for that look small. Incidentally, I was almost skipper of a swell diesel-electric tug, but the orders for my present job came through before our commanding officer could put me on the tug. Perhaps I wouldn't have been so good on there, but surely would have enjoyed it, and think that if I could have worked under a skipper who knew something about it for a little while, I think I could have done all right. Those boats handle so very easily – and I know I could have done as well as the fellow they finally had to put on that tug. Oh well, maybe I'll get a chance at something better.

Have you been kept busy lately? I imagine that the oil business is slowing down some now. Sometimes I wish I was back working on the number 18.

Well, I must try to write answers to some of the other letters I received. My love to Mother, Violet and yourself.

Your son,
Arne

P.S. I am enclosing a paper which should enable you to cash the check. I don't imagine there will be any more for I think that one was just for my uniform allowance. I am sending money home by

money order instead of allotments from Washington – it is just as safe, and faster, and if I ever need money for an emergency I will be able to draw it, which I couldn't if I made out an allotment.
The news bulletin below occurred while I was writing this letter.

AMPHIBIOUS FORCE – NW AFRICAN WATERS,
                    MAY 10, 1943
SATURDAY NIGHT. GERMAN FRONT IS TONIGHT RAPIDLY DISINTEGRATING. GERMAN AND ITALIANS ARE IN CONFUSION AND DISORDER. THEIR LAST DEFENSE LINES ARE CRUMBLING. AXIS TROOPS ARE FALLING BACK DEFEATED AND DISORGANISED WITH LITTLE CHANCE OF MAKING ANOTHER STAND. THOUSANDS OF PRISONERS ESTIMATED TO RUN INTO FIVE FIGURES ARE ALREADY IN ALLIED HANDS. BRITISH TANKS WHICH ENTERED TUNIS FRIDAY PRESSED ON TO SOUTHEAST YESTERDAY AND ARE MILLING AROUND IN AREA THROUGH WHICH RETREATING GERMANS MUST SLIP TO REACH CAPE DON PENINSULA.

BIZERTA: LORRY AFTER LORRY PASSED BY ROAD CARRYING GERMAN PRISONERS. AMERICAN ARMOUR GOT BEHIND HILL NORTH EAST OF MATURE AT DUSK THURSDAY STARTING AVALANCHE OF PRISONERS DOWN SLOPES. AFTER THE BATTLE WHOLE HILLSIDES WERE COVERED WITH GERMAN DEAD AND WOUNDED. MORE PRISONERS STREAMED THROUGH VILLAGES ON FRIDAY AS TANKS DROVE NORTHWARD. REUTERS CORRESPONDENT REPORTS CHEERING CROWDS LINED FERRYVILLE STREETS THROWING ROSES ON OUR JEEP, SHAKING HANDS AND CLIMBING ABOARD. BOTH MEN AND WOMEN KISSING ME AND OTHER CORRESPONDENTS. THEY ASKED FOR NEWS OF BIZERTA AND TUNIS AND YELLED HYSTERICALLY AS THEY RELAYED NEWS OF ALLIES AND RAPID PUSH. TRICOLORS WERE EVERYWHERE.

                    MAY 11, 1943
TUNIS: REUTERS CORRESPONDENT IN NORTHWEST AFRICA DESCRIBES TUNIS AIRPORT AS SCENE OF TOTAL DESTRUCTION IN ONE CORNER OF WHICH IS "MORTUARY" OF JUNKERS, FORTY TWO TROOP CARRIERS, SOME NEARLY NEW. THE CITY OF TUNIS ITSELF IS PRACTICALLY UNDAMAGED BY BOMBS BUT DOCKS AT TUNIS AND LA

27

GOULETTE ARE SHAMBLES. MOST OF WRECKS ARE AT LA
GOULETTE WHERE SEVERAL SHIPS WERE STILL BURNING.
NEAR SHORE A LARGE ITALIAN SHIP WAS AGROUND FROM
WHICH SMALL BOATS WERE BRINGING TO BEACH BRITISH
AND AMERICAN PRISONERS OF WAR.

Downed Junkers

Another downed German plane

Northwest Africa
May 16, 1943

Dear Mom, Dad, & Violet,

I've received quite a bit of mail from you recently. Altogether, I've had 17 letters from you since I got here almost three months ago. And I imagine there must be more on the way. Two days ago, I received your letter dated May 5th, and that really is fast time – just 9 days.

I'm sorry to hear Aleck is worried about his standing in the Air Corps, but I think he will make it. Didn't he feel the same way a couple of times in preflight, and primary schools? Seems to me he did.

Today I went to church – in the tent chapel. Mike is really a fine preacher, and I'm glad to have him as a friend. He is getting a new chapel pretty soon – a large tin-roofed hut, which will also be used as a recreation hall. That will be pretty nice, don't you think?

Today I got some more clothes. I was issued 3 khaki shirts and two trousers. They are better than the ones I bought – made for Army officers, but are almost exactly like ours in looks. So now I don't have to worry about a shortage of clothes. Have you received my letter requesting a package yet? I hope so. Some of the things I asked for could be used very well now. I also sent, in a letter to you, Dad, the power of attorney necessary to cash my check – you should have that pretty soon now.

Yesterday, I was put on the night watch – on duty from midnight to 8 AM. It isn't bad, for there isn't much to do and I got a little chance to think and write. The only trouble is that in our quarters, there are 5 fellows, and it is a little hard to get any sleep during the day. Somebody is always coming in or going out, or talking. Well, I'll get used to it.

Here's a little poem I wrote not so long ago.

Meditation
The one who talks with Jesus
When he is sore opprest,
Will find relief and succor,
And know His way is best.

29

Not only when you're troubled,
But when you're happy too,
He's always sympathetic,
When He belongs to you.

My love to the best family in the world.
Arne

Dear Mom & Dad,

I'm so very thankful that all your mail is coming through so well, and it seems like my mail has been arriving home all right too. I'm glad you got my money orders. Did you get the second hundred dollars I sent you yet?

It is nice to hear that you get a letter from Virginia once in a while – I think it is very thoughtful of her. Do you still have the same opinion of her you had last September, Mom? She said she is sending me a small gold cross and chain to wear around my neck. Isn't that pretty swell?

It may be that I won't be able to write as often from now on, for I am going to be very busy. However, I will try and write whenever possible, and if you don't hear for a while, please don't worry – I'll be all right.

Did I tell you we have a couple of barn swallows living in our room? They have hatched some eggs, and are just as proud as can be. They scurry around all day long to feed their young ones – and sing all the while. Their song is very similar to that of a canary, but not quite as well developed.

It is getting warmer every day. When we first arrived, we used to use four blankets at night – now two is plenty, and soon one should be enough.

Mother, it wasn't necessary to send the white shirts – for when they come they will just be tucked away in my bag. I have only worn one white shirt since leaving, and that was the one I had on the morning I left. I am eagerly waiting for my package to arrive for I can certainly use that material.

Say, I'm getting to be quite a poet. Here is another set of verses I wrote recently.

Morning Prayer
"Tis always darkest 'fore the dawn"
Somebody used to say –
But when the light of early morn
Breaks into shining day
And dispels every trace of storm,
We lift our hearts to pray.

31

"Dear Lord, we thank Thee for this night,
    For e'en though storm winds blow
We know we were within Thy sight,
    And Thou would see us through.
To bring us safely into light,
    We thank Thee all anew."

Hope Aleck is doing all right – and that everything at home is fine. Love to you all,

                                                                    Arne

The warning regarding fewer letters had to do with an upcoming move to Bizerte and Tunis/LaGoulette. There was much packing and arranging for the LST voyage from Arzew to Bizerte. This took 4 or 5 days. We arrived in Bizerte and stayed a few days, then went by jeep and truck convoy to Tunis. Picture to the left shows me in one of the jeeps. On the way we saw these remnants of Roman Aqueducts.

Jensen in a jeep to Tunis

Arab fellow travelers

Entering Tunis 28 May, 1943

Ancient Roman Aqueduct ruins

North Africa,
May 30, 1943

Dear Mom & Dad & Violet,

    I'm sorry I haven't been able to write sooner, but I have been very busy. I have been moved to a different location which in a way is better than the old place. Seems to be improving all the time. My new work is very interesting and I enjoy it a lot. There is so much to learn – seems like I'll never get it all. Incidentally, I think it might be well to change my address:

        Ens. A Jensen, USNR
        Navy 1940 *(for LaGoulette)*
        c/o Fleet Post Office
        New York, N.Y.

    The country we are in now is somewhat the same – drab, windy, dusty – but there are many interesting things to see. There are ruins nearby which are thousands of years old. *(This refers to Carthage.)* Oh, if I only had some more film for my camera. The people in this part of the country are about the same – they don't seem to vary much.

    We are eating well, and keeping in good health. Our drinking water has to be chlorinated – which gives it a flat, unpleasant taste, but we get around that by making lemonade, and drinking coffee. I haven't had a chance to weigh myself lately, but last time I was around 155 lbs., and my trousers are a little tighter now than then so I might very well be up to 160 lbs. Anyway, you don't have to worry about your big boy – he is getting along fine. I have accumulated some laundry and must try and wash it sometime soon. Laundry facilities here are not too good, and the best way is to do as much of it yourself as possible. I'll have to find a barber soon too. Last time I had a haircut was about a month ago, and now it is pretty long (my hair, of course).

    I know there are about 4 or 5 people in Africa that I remember from the States, but I have only come across one so far. Will you tell Aleck that I saw Red Mackay over here (I don't think you knew him, but maybe you did). I just got to say hello and that is all. Tried to locate him later, but was unable to do so. Well, it's getting late again, and I must retire – we get up about 6:30 AM

34

here All my love to you folks.
Keep smiling,

Arne

North Africa
June 6, 1943

Dear Mom & Dad & Violet,

This must be a very short note – it's past midnight and I'm tired and sleepy. There has been a mail call three times in the last four days – but nothing for me. Haven't had any mail now for three weeks, and I was getting it regularly before that. Must be held up somewhere along the line. Haven't received your package yet, either.

Took a shower and sun bath on the roof today – made me

Rooftop View

feel like a new man. The view from the roof is beautiful. There are rugged mountains in the distance – a beautiful town on a nearby hill, and the town spread out around us.

There is a swell* beach nearby, but I haven't had a chance to go swimming yet – much too busy. Hope to get a chance soon.

The term 'swell' was very common in the '40s and '50s, and was equivalent to 'cool' in later generations. The picture may not be the scene I was referring to, but is a typical view from the roof of our quarters.

Here's a little poem I wrote not so long ago.

> A Prayer
> Oh God, Creator of the earth,
> Draw near this troubled land;
> Oh Thou who made us, gave us birth,
> We need Thy guiding hand.
>
> We need Thy boundless mercy free,
> Forgiveness for our sins,
> We need Thy grace to make us see
> Where Thy great love begins.
>
> Oh Lord, we are but frail and weak,
> And prone to go astray.
> Therefore from Thee our strength we seek,
> We know Thou'lt hear us pray.

All my love to the best family a fellow could have.

Arne

Large V-mail form
June 11, 1943
Dear Mom & Dad & Violet,

How is everything at home? I haven't received any mail now for four weeks, and keep wondering when I'll hear from you. Your package hasn't arrived yet, although I know it is somewhere in Africa because a friend of mine at another base told me he had seen it. It will probably get here pretty soon. I haven't drawn any pay since the first part of May, so I have quite a bit coming. As soon as I can I will draw some and send it on home. Did you get the second hundred dollars I sent the early part of May? Hope you did.

My friend, the Chaplain, came down for a visit today – it was nice to see him again. He is rather lonesome and homesick for the States and his wife, but then who isn't? I'd like to get back soon too. Can't tell, it might be soon, but then again it might be longer than we think. Well, time will tell.

How is Aleck doing? He didn't wash out of basic did he? Hope not. And how is everybody else? Sure hope I get some mail soon.

Love to all,
Arne

This tells the sad story

North Africa
13 June, 1943

Dear Dad,

Just a little letter to let you know I am thinking of you on Father's Day. We are having nice weather, but it is really getting warm. I can imagine what it will be like during the summer.

There is a beach not far away – where we can go

swimming. I haven't gone yet – too many other things to do. However, I am going very soon. Some of the fellows have gone and have said that it is swell.

Yesterday I did a large washing – underwear, socks, towels, pajamas & handkerchiefs.

(Nearby Beach)

It took all afternoon, but now I have some clean clothes to put away. It doesn't come out as nice and white as Mom's washing, but that's because we haven't any bleach, and the water is quite hard. I have to send out my khaki trousers & shirts – they are too hard to do without an iron.

I am including a few pictures for the family. They are not too good, but that is because the man who processed the film did not have good materials – and I can tell he wasn't very careful either. But they are nice to have & will be a remembrance of my days in Africa.

I still haven't had any mail – it is over a month now – and I'm getting a little blue. Perhaps I'll get some tonight. I know Mother's package is over here, but still haven't received it.

I looked in my account book just a little while ago and discovered that so far this year, I've earned a little over a thousand dollars – that's pretty good, isn't it? Boy, what an income tax I'm going to have to pay when I come back!

I hope everyone at home is feeling good – and for you, on Father's Day, I wish you all the health and happiness possible for many, many years to come. Love from your son,

Arne

P.S. Kiss Mom & Violet for me.

39

(Large V-mail form)
June, 15, 1943
Dear Mom & Dad,

Yesterday I received a most pleasant surprise – 7 letters. I had two from you, two from Virginia, two from Loren, and one from Jean Anne. It was swell to hear from you all. And today I received the package of cookies and a large picture Virginia sent about two months ago. As yet, I haven't received your package, but expect I will get it any day now. I was very sorry to hear that Aleck washed out of pilot training – personally I think it's the Army's loss – but maybe it happened for the best. He probably will try for navigator's school now, won't he? It is rather warm here tonight – I took my shirt off to try and keep cool.

Yesterday, I did quite a bit of laundry – underwear, socks, etc. I also sent some more out – costs about the same as in the States.

Monday will be pay day – I think – and if possible, I will draw all I have coming and send it home to you. There should be about $250 in my pay account now. Well, it will all go in the bank – best place for it.

Must say good-night, for it's rather late.

All my love,
Arne

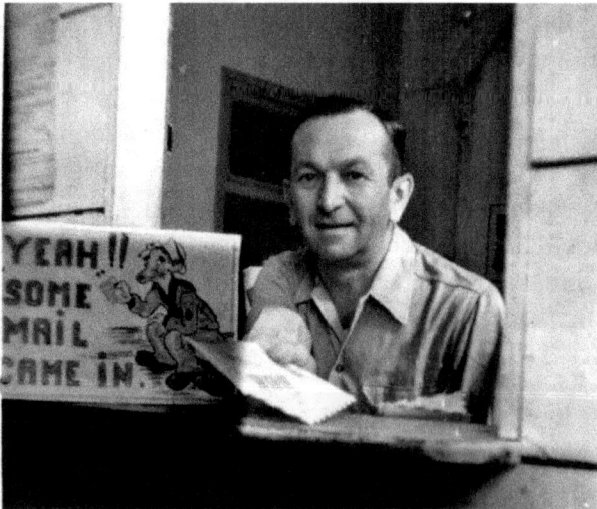

Oh happy mail day!

Dear Mom,

I have received 3 letters from you and two from Dad in the last week or so – and it was so very welcome. I had quite a few other letters too – guess I told you about that before. In one of the letters I had from Virginia, she included a small gold cross and chain which I am now wearing around my neck. I think it is beautiful and think it was really thoughtful of her to send it to me. Don't you?

I was sorry to hear about all the sickness the Lindberg's have had – seems that someone in their family is always sick. I will try to write them soon – but I have so many letters to answer right now that it won't be for a week or so.

I can't understand why your package hasn't arrived yet – I think it should have been here before this because a friend of mine saw it at the last station I was at over 2 weeks ago. Well, it will turn up sometime soon.

I'm glad to hear Violet is doing so well in her school work – as a matter of fact, I think she is doing much better than her brothers ever did. Sure hope that she gets to college someday – I think she could really go places in some science line.

How do you like my poems, Mom? You're never said anything about them so sometimes I wonder if you have received them yet. I have written quite a number since I've been over here – it is one way of expressing myself. And I get a feeling of satisfaction in being able to write something like that. Show them to Pastor Okdale sometime, and if he thinks they are good enough, he can use them in any way he sees fit. Here is one I wrote yesterday.

The Little Things

The many, many little things
Which don't amount to much,
A cheerful word, the song one sings,
A little gift, and such.

41

A flower for the one who's sick,
A laughing, twinkling eye,
Just one of these will do the trick -
Dispel a care or sigh.

And if you add them – what a sum
It finally will be!
Believe me, it will soon become
A wondrous sight to see.

That one is the fourth I will have sent you when this letter goes in the mail. I have some more that I will send in later letters.

Again, it is time to close – so until next time, "Keep smiling", and greet everyone for me. Love to Violet & Dad.

All my love,
Arne

Around the Base
at
AATB
La Goulette,
Tunis

Arne and Mike

View of LaGoulette

Flag flying on top of the Administration building

Enlisted men's club

Guard on duty at warehouse

Radiomen at a 'picnic' feed

LaGoulette street scene

Large V-mail form
June 21, 1943
Dear Dad,

      I am answering your letters by air mail today, because I don't have much time to spare. We are kept quite busy all the time – and what free time we have is devoted to laundry, eating, sleeping, etc. I am glad to hear that you finally got my check cashed and deposited in the bank. Was hoping to be paid today, but it looks like I'll have to wait another two weeks or so. When payday does come, I should have quite a bit coming and will send as much as possible home. Have you read of or heard anything about servicemen being forgiven all of their 1943 income tax as well as that of 1942? There have been some rumors here to that effect.

      Would you have Mother send me Aleck's new address if he has moved? I am very anxious to hear how he is doing and to keep in touch with him. It's nice to hear the fellows at Poling's are asking for me. Send them my best regards. And to Mother and Violet all my love & kisses.

Love from your son,

Arne

Poling Brothers Oil Transportation Co. was the outfit Dad worked for, and I had worked with him as a deckhand during college summers and the month of January '43 , before being called up for active duty.

Dear Mom,

At last I received your package – many thanks. I had just about given up all hope of ever seeing it, but yesterday it came. The silver dog tag chain was swell – now I am all set on that score – and the penknife and nail clippers – and to top it all off, the four rolls of film. I bought a roll of French film the other day and it cost $1.60 – what do you think of that? When my friend brought the package up to me, all the fellows congregated around to see me open it. But to kid them a little, I didn't bother with it, just kept on working. Then they became disappointed, so I had to open it and show them what I got. It's funny, they all thought it was food of some sort – waited around to get a share of it. No need telling you the chocolate didn't last very long. The flashlight glass was a little cracked in one corner, and a little banged up (but it works) – I wonder if that happened on the way over, or whether it was like that?

The weather over here continues to be beautiful – clear, sunny days, cool nights – perfect for sleeping. They say that California has weather very similar to this. However, it is the kind of climate that makes you lazy – even though it's nice.

I had a very nice letter from Anna Knutsen a couple of days ago – she tells me she has another job now. She also told me a little about Roy (but nothing concerning that secret). She writes a very nice letter, and I hope she writes again.

You haven't given me any news about Alcck for a while now – how is he getting along? Where is he, and what is he doing? I suppose Violet is out on vacation now – having a good time. Has she got a boy-friend yet?

The other day I washed all my bed clothes – got the sheets and pillow case quite white (I was surprised). If I only had a little more ambition, I'd do all my clothes too. But it's quite a job when you have to do it all by hand and there is no hot water unless we heat a pail (and that is rather hard to do).

Next payday I will have about $400 coming – what do you think of that? And as I wrote Dad, the income tax has been practically wiped out for lower grade servicemen, so all I make is clear profit so to speak. By the end of the year, I should have a good sized bank account. Incidentally, I will enclose that slip from the bank in this letter.

Well, back to work I must go – a hug and kiss for all of you until next time.

All my love,
Arne

Base Dry Dock
One of the reasons for our existence, dry dock repair
of amphibious landing craft, a very important part of our
"Reason for being" and a significant reason for the choice of the
base's location. As you may deduce, a ship with hull damage loves
going into a dry dock (when water in it permits entry). When
properly aligned and tied up, the water is drained out and the dock
becomes 'dry' and hull repair can begin. The picture above shows
a tug boat in for repair work.

The letter below is a copy of an actual typed letter. I was very busy in the Communications Office, and using the ECM machine as a letter writing typewriter. A fuller description of the ECM machine is an insertion to the May 8th letter. Note that it only typed capital letters, no lower case..

I must point out here that the several complaints about heavy work load were due to the increasing closeness to the start of the Sicilian invasion, "Operation Husky", on July 17. There was a brief slowing of radio traffic because all ships involved had to observe 'radio silence'. After the start of the invasion, radio traffic shot up and we were busy again.

DEAR MOM, DAD AND VIOLET,

IN THE MIDST OF A MESS OF WORK I AM TAKING OFF A FEW MINUTES TO DROP YOU A FEW LINES. WE ARE VERY BUSY--AS YOU NO% DOUBT CAN IMAGINE. I HAVEN'T RECEIVED MUCH MAIL LATELY ALTHOUGH I DID GET A LETTER FROM YOU ABOUT FOUR OR FIVE DAYS AGO. I ALSO RECEIVED THE SENTINEL FROM HELEN BJERTNESS--WHICH WAS A PLEASANT SURPRISE. IT WAS SWELL TO HEAR THAT ALBEE GOT HIS WINGS AND COMMISSION.

HOW IS ALECK DOING? EVERY LETTER I GET I LOOK FOR NEWS ABOUT HIM, BUT IN THE LAST FEW LETTERS THERE HASN'T BEEN ANY-THING.

IT IS VERY WARM HERE RIGHT NOW. WHILE WE ARE WORKING WE HAVE TO REMOVE OUR SHIRTS OTHERWISE THEY GET SOAKED RIGHT THROUGH. I SUPPOSE IT IS QUITE WARM IN NEW YORK TOO. ARE YOU FOLKS GOING TO TAKE A VACATION THIS YEAR? IF YOU POSSIBLY CAN YOU SHOULD.

HAVE YOU RECEIVED THE PICTURES I SENT YOU YET? THEY SHOULD BE HOME BY NOW. AS SOON AS I CAN HAVE THE REST OF MY FILMS DEVELOPED I SHALL SEND THEM ALONG TO YOU.

OH - OH, HERE COMES SOME BUSINESS--I BETTER SIGN OFF FOR THIS TIME--WILL TRY TO WRITE A FEW LINES AGAIN SOON.

ALL MY LOVE,

July 6, 1943
North Africa

Dear Mom,

Had a letter from you tonight, and also one from Alma. Yours was dated June 8th and Alma's was from June 11. I can't quite figure out why our mail is taking so long to get here – we were getting mail in 14 days and less. And I am still getting all my mail addressed to the first base I was at, and I haven't been there since May 3rd – isn't that funny?

I was glad to get the copy of the bulletin with my poem in it – I still don't think they are so good, but if Pastor Okdale wants to use them it's all right with me. Have you received the others I sent you yet?

How about Aleck, Mom – how is he doing? I am very anxious to know how he is making out, and there hasn't been much news about him in your latest letters. Is he still in pilot training school or did he wash out?

Mom, I must compliment you on the fine job of writing you are doing* – both in the sense of volume, and quality. Your spelling is almost perfect and your punctuation is just as good. And all the little newsy items about all the people I know is just grand to get. And I must say the same about Dad's letters. Seems to me I wrote Violet a letter, but I haven't heard from her yet. How about giving her a little push?

It has been very warm here lately – the thermometer has been above 100 all day, and in the evening it isn't much cooler. Hope this heat wave breaks soon, but we don't have very high hopes on that score.

My eyes are very heavy, and I should hit the sack. All my love and regards to Dad and Violet.

Love,
Arne

*My mother grew up on a farm in Norway and had to walk 2 miles to school. She completed third grade and then was told by her father that she was needed at the farm for chores; that was the end of her formal education. However, she continued to read and was self taught even after arriving in America. She did amazingly well writing in English, with only a few 'phonic' misspellings.

Another news clip below.

27 JULY, 1943
THE SUCCESSOR TO MUSSOLINI'S CROWN, SEVENTY THREE
YEAR OLD MARSHAL BADOGLIO, HAS OPPOSED BENITO
MUSSOLINI SINCE THE START OF THE FASCIST REGIME.
BADOGLIO IS A CLOSE FRIEND OF THE KING AND ALWAYS
REPRESENTED THE ROYALIST VIEWPOINT.
ALLIED HQ IN NORTH AFRICA: AMERICAN INFANTRY AND
TANKS SWEPT ALONG THE NORTH COAST OF SICILY
MONDAY IN CLOSE PURSUIT OF THE ITALIAN MILITARY
RABBLE FALLING BACK WITH HARDLY A FIGHT TOWARD
THE MESSINA BRIDGEHEAD. MARSHAL BADOGLIO'S
RESUMPTION OF COMMAND UNDER KING EMANUELE
CAUSED NO PAUSE IN THE FLIGHT OF REMNANTS OF HIS
SICILIAN GARRISON.

Actual V-Mail as sent and received by photographic means. The original was scanned for this book.
See next page for picture of the Cathedral

No.

[CENSOR'S STAMP]

To MRS. KARL G. JENSEN
825 7Ø STREET
BROOKLYN, N.Y.
NEW YORK

From ENS. A. JENSEN, USNR
(Sender's name)
NAVY 94 C/O F.P.O.
(Sender's address)
NEW YORK, NEW YORK
JULY 17, 1943
(Date)

DEAR MOTHER,

IT IS NOW 2 AM AND I AM PREPARING TO GO TO BED. YOU SEE I NOW HAVE THE LATE WATCH, AND HAVE TO STAY UP UNTIL ALL THE DAYS BUSINESS IS CLEANED UP. AND THEN I GET TO SLEEP LATE IN THE MORNING -- AND THAT IS ALL RIGHT FOR I ALWAYS DID LIKE THAT, REMEMBER?

EVERYTHING IS GOING ALONG NICELY HERE -- I AM FEELING FINE, AND EXCEPT FOR BEING A LITTLE HOMESICK, I AM ENJOYING MYSELF. THERE ISN'T MUCH TO DO FOR ENTERTAINMENT AS IVE SAID BEFORE, BUT WE MANAGE TO AMUSE OURSELVES SOMEHOW. YESTERDAY EVENING WE TOOK A LITTLE TRIP AROUND THE COUNTRYSIDE IN A JEEP AND HAD A LOT OF FUN. WE SAW A CATHEDRAL WHICH IS FAIRLY OLD. IT WAS VERY ORNATE AND ELABORATE INSIDE WITH MOSAICS AND STAINED GLASS WINDOWS. PERSONNALY, I PREFER THE SIMPLICITY OF BETHANY TO SOMETHING LIKE THAT. THEN WE PASSED THROUGH AN ARAB VILLAGE -- SAW HOW THE ARABS LIVED -- I'LL TAKE THE GODD OLD AMERICAN WAY FIRST, LAST AND ALWAYS. THE LITTLE KIDS FOLLOWED US AROUND ASKING FOR CANDY AND BON-BONS. SOME OF THEM WERE KINDA CUTE, BUT OTHERS WERE NOT SO NICE.

I RECEIVED A LETTER FROM YOU AND ONE FROM DAD YESTERDAY -- THANKS SO MUCH. WILL WRITE TO DAD VERY SOON. HAVEN'T BEEN ABLE TO GET TO A MONEY ORDER STATION YET BUT WILL TRY TO FIND ONE TOMORROW. PAYDAY AGAIN TODAY BUT I DIDN'T NEED ANY MONEY SO I LEFT IT ON THE BOOKS.

MY EYES ARE BEGINNING TO CLOSE SO WILL SAY GOOD NIGHT FOR NOW. REGARDS TO DAD AND VIOLET AND PASS ON MY GREETINGS TO ALECK.

LOVE,

This picture was taken in 1943. It is the Cathedral of St. George.

Checking with Google, I found it was a Greek Orthodox Cathedral.

As you can see, at that time there was lots of open land around it,

but now, 2014, the city of Tunis has grown out and around it. The close up picture was copied from the Internet and shows a front view of the Cathedral. The travel company description of the interior is not informative in terms of seating capacity, although it did say the pews had cushions, and the interior was spacious. There were many wood carvings and painting of saints on the walls.

You will also notice that palm trees have been planted in front of the cathedral.

Actual V-mail as typed; this one came by air mail. Scanned

No. _____

(CENSOR'S STAMP)

To MR KARL G. JENSEN

825 7Ø STREET

BROOKLYN, NEW YORK

NEW YORK

From
ENS. A JENSEN, USNR
(Sender's name)

NAVY 94 C/O F. P. O.
(Sender's address)

NEW YORK, NEW YORK

JULY 19, 1943
(Date)

DEAR DAD,

IT WAS SO NICE TO GET YOUR LETTER OF JUNE 22. GOLLY, IT MAKES A
FELLOW REALLY FEEL GOOD TO KNOW THE FOLKS BACK HOME ARE BACKING HIM UP
WITH THEIR THOUGHTS AND PRAYERS. I'M SORRY YOU HADN'T HEARD FROM ME FOR
SO LONG BUT IT WAS UNAVOIDABLE FOR I WAS BEING MOVED AT THE TIME AND THERE
WAS NO WAY OF GETTING LETTERS MAILED.   I THINK IT WOULD BE NICE IF YOU
COULD GET TO TAKE THE NUMBER TEN DOWN TO MIAMI -- IT WOULD OR SHOULD BE A
NICE TRIP -- WISH I COULD MAKE IT WITH YOU.   I'M VERY SORRY TO HEAR THAT
ALECK DIDN'T PASS HIS PILOTS EXAMINATION -- PERSONALLY I THINK HE WOULD
HAVE BEEN A GOOD ONE, BUT THEN MAYBE HE WILL BE BETTER AS A NAVIGATOR.
IT WOULD BE NICE FOR HIM IF HE DOES GET A FURLOUGH -- HE REALLY DESERVES
IT AFTER ALL THAT HARD WORK IN FLYING SCHOOL.   SO ANDY AND LANNIGAN ARE
STILL WITH YOU -- WELL I EXPECTED THEM TO, BUT THOUGHT PERHAPS THEY MIGHT
TAKE ONE OF THEM. DO YOU SUPPOSE I COULD GET A JOB WITH THE POLINGS AGAIN
IF NOTHING ELSE IS AVAILABLE WHEN I GET BACK? OF COURSE I WOULD ONLY DO
THAT AS A LAST RESORT, AND CHANCES ARE I WOULD NEVER HAVE TO DO IT.
TALK ABOUT YOUR HEAT -- WE HAVE BEEN HAVING TEMPERATURES OF 1ØØ DEGREES
AND OVER ALMOST EVERY DAY FOR QUITE SOME TIME NOW -- BUT WE GET USED TO IT
AFTER A BIT. SOMETIMES THE WIND FEELS LIKE A BLAST RIGHT OUT OF THE FURNACE
AND YOU CAN IMAGINE WHAT THAT WOULD BE LIKE. HOWEVER, IT IS FAIRLY DRY SO
WE DON'T SUFFER VERY MUCH.   SURE COULD GO FOR AN ICE CREAM SODA RIGHT NOW.
MUST CLOSE -- ALL MY LOVE TO YOU, MOTHER, VIOLET, AND ALECK AND ALL THE
OTHERS I KNOW.

V----MAIL

Tunisia, North Africa
(Now permitted regional location identification)
July 23, 1943

Dear Mom,

I finally got to a post office and bought some money orders. I'm going to include one order for $100 in this letter and $100 in each of the next 2 letters, making a total of $300. The reason I'm sending them in separate letters is, that if one letter gets lost, we won't lose all the money. And you take care of the money the way we planned.

By the way, has my bill at Macy's been all paid up yet? If not, finish it up by taking it out of my share of this money. And did I tell you that I had two allotments made out? One is to you – for $100 to be treated the same as these money orders. It will probably start coming from Washington the end of August or the beginning of September. The other allotment is for me $25 war bond per month made out to me but sent to you for safekeeping. You are named as beneficiary on the war bonds. That should also start coming about the same time as the other one.

Today we had rain – first time since April – and was it refreshing. It only lasted a few minutes but was really welcome.

The British news broadcasts have been encouraging lately. Things are looking up – sure hope we can finish up over here soon and go back home. Don't imagine we will for a while yet though.

The mail hasn't been coming through so good lately. Sometimes I wonder how it is coming in on your end. Hope you are getting all my letters. Things are much the same here – working quite a bit – have the late shift. Get up around 11 AM in time for lunch. Yesterday afternoon I washed my sheets & pillow case. Think I did a pretty good job, but wish we had hot water and a bleach like Clorox. That would make it much easier. When I do my washing, I take my shirt off – and now I have a pretty good tan – in fact, I have a little burn.

We have the swellest bunch of officers and men in our department. We all get along well – and have a lot of fun while we work. And I am feeling better now than I have felt in years. Haven't had a cold or sniffle since April – and you remember, I always used to have a sniffle. So you see, there is nothing to worry about – only thing wrong is that I miss the States & wish I was back. And there's nothing to be done about that.

55

Well, there are a few more letters to be written, so will close for now. All my love to Dad, Violet, & Aleck.

Love,

Arne

*Here I will add a story **not** for telling family at that time. After several months we had a minor medical problem: Both enlisted men and officers came down with "the runs". For me it lasted 10 days and I lost 10 pounds and became very familiar with the route to the "Head" (Navy term for the toilet). The base doctor finally diagnosed the problem as amoebic dysentery. The cause? Our mess hall had screens with unpatched holes, and the screen door was often left open. Also, mess personnel would set out flatware and glasses right after the dish washer was done. It was obvious to the doctor what had to be done: patch the holes, install self-closing door hardware, and mess men were not to set the tables until just before a meal. This prevented the e-coli laden flies from depositing their cargo on our tableware. There was a gradual recovery and subsequently it was rare that anyone showed up at 'sick call' with that kind of complaint.*

Tunisia, North Africa
July 31, 1943

Dear Mom & Dad,

I've received 4 of your letters within the last five days, and I really feel good when I get them. I'm sorry I haven't been able to write any sooner, but these 18 hour days don't leave much time for writing. We have been extremely busy lately. It is now 2:45 AM and I have just about finished my work – getting ready to go to bed.

Your mail is finally coming thru to the correct address – in approximately two weeks, and it ought to be better as time goes by. How long does it take for my mail to get home?

Did you get my last letter with the $100 money order in it? I hope so. I am enclosing another $100 in this one – and in my next letter there will be another and in the one after that there ought to be another, unless I forget. Oh yes, I must tell you that my allotments won't start until September, so you probably won't start getting the checks until the end of that month. Boy, I'll really have a lot of money saved up when I get home.

The news has been very good lately – it looks like Italy will soon be out of the war – and then perhaps it won't be long, after that – and we can go home. *(Frequent wishful thinking)*

Hope you don't mind my closing now – my eyes can hardly stay open. Will try to write again soon.

Good night and love to you all, Arne

3 AUGUST 1943

ITALIANS ARE WARNED: A SPECIAL MESSAGE WAS BROADCAST TO THE ITALIAN PEOPLE LAST NIGHT FROM ALGIERS RADIO. THE MESSAGE STATED THAT ALLIED TROOPS WOULD SOON BE FIGHTING ON THE ITALIAN MAINLAND. "WE HAVE AWAITED THE DECISION OF THE ITALIAN PEOPLE FOR EIGHT DAYS. OUR FORCES ARE NOW ON THE MOVE AND AT YOUR VERY GATES. YOU WILL INEVITABLY SUFFER ALL THE HORRORS OF WAR---WAR ON THE ITALIAN PENINSULA. OUR FORCES ARE IRRESISTABLE."

Tunisia, North Africa
Aug. 5, 1943

Dear Mom & Dad & Violet,

Have had a number of letters from you in the last week – but I have been unable to write any letters myself. This evening I am taking some time off to drop you a few lines and to send you my third $100 money order. My next letter will contain the fourth one.

Just balanced my books the other day, and in the first half of 1943, I've received $1187.73 – that's pretty good isn't it? By the end of this year, I will have made about $2400 – I'll really be rich pretty soon. My savings are increasing very satisfactorily, and I've paid you folks back quite a bit – with more to come. Perhaps you are saving that as a nest egg – maybe as a down payment on a house, yes? It's a good idea anyway.

The heat here has been terrific – we remove almost all our clothes (except our trousers) while we work in the office. We have received an extra typewriter and a typist lately – so that will take part of the load off us. We still are working quite long hours – but we don't mind so much – for it is interesting work.
(Interesting work indeed, deciphering and reading 'Top Secret' messages!)

Took a business trip to a nearby base *(most likely Bizerte)* a few days ago. After finishing my business, I saw my friend Mike Silseth, the chaplain, and we went swimming. It was on the most beautiful beach. It reminded me a lot of Sandve in Norway – remember when we took that trip – we still have pictures of it with cousins Alf & Bendik, Aleck & I running around with nothing on*. This beach had the cleanest, white sand, and the water was clean, and clear. We had a good time.

The picture on the next page (circa 1922) was taken from an old Family album and shows the four of us, Alf, Bendik, Aleck and me, in our 'birthday suits'.

The news gets better every day – Sicily can't hold out more than a few days – and then pretty soon Italy will fold up too. I surely hope

(Photo circa 1922 at Sandvesanden beach, Norway

this war will be finished soon. We get the news by radio from London – so we manage to keep up with things pretty well.*)*

Must close now – as a postlude, here is a little poem – it's not so good in poetical form, but you won't mind that, I'm sure.

A Prayer
In shame and sorrow for my sins,
I turn to Thee my Lord;
In meek repentance, ask of Thee
The blessings of Thy Work.
The wicked, evil life I've led,
I shamefully confess;
Please hear my prayer – and heal my soul,
In Thy mercifulness.

All my love to you at home. Keep smiling!
Arne

P.S. Please let me know when you receive the money orders and also the numbers (if you haven't cashed them already) so I can check if they are lost.

Tunisia, North Africa
Aug. 8, 1943

Dear Mom,

Another letter from you today – dated July 23 – the mail is beginning to come thru faster now. At last it is coming directly to the base I'm at. That, of course, makes a big difference.

I was surprised to hear Carl Bergman is engaged – and also surprised to hear Jimmy & Albee got "hooked". I thought Jimmy was overseas – did he get back home or was I imagining things?

You shouldn't wait till we come home to go to the country – I think Dad & Violet were wise in wanting to go. Of course, I know how you feel – but it may be quite a while before we get home, and you should take every opportunity, for it may be even more difficult later.

This afternoon Smitty and I went swimming with another fellow. We had lots of fun – but the water was kind of salt. We took a shower afterward, which was very refreshing.

You know, the officer in charge of our division, Lieutenant Long, is a fine man to work for. He sees that we are kept with all the supplies necessary, gets right down and helps us if we are very busy, and in general is "one of the boys". It makes it very pleasant that way – we have 5 fine officers and 11 fine men in our division – and we all get along swell.

I am sending the <u>fourth</u> and last of a series of $100 money orders in this letter – hope you have received the others by now. Please let me know when you get them, and the serial numbers on them. I'll probably send you another one the first part of September, and after that, you will receive that money by allotment direct from Washington, the first one near the end of September or the beginning of October and every month thereafter. You will also receive a $25 war bond in my name, with you as the beneficiary – for safekeeping. By next year, I should have quite a sizable sum saved up, and you will have been repaid quite a bit of what I borrowed from you in school. Maybe I will have enough to get married on when I get back – do you think?

I'm way behind in my letter writing, and there never seems to be enough time to get caught up. Oh well, sooner or later I will catch up.

Say how about Violet dropping me a line? And how is she doing in school? Is she still taking piano lessons – I hope?

We have been getting some good food over here – for a change. Today we had pork chops and boiled potatoes & spinach & cake. Yesterday we had roast veal with all the trimmings. We get the news every day – and lately it has been very good. Perhaps we will see the end of this frightful war soon, but I'm afraid it is going to last another year anyway. Well, all we can do is hope & pray.

I'm on the late shift again this week – will work until about 3-4 AM. It's not so bad – I kinda like it.

Must try to write a few more letters now – so until next time – all my love to you all at home – and God bless you.

Arne

This picture really belongs on the next letter page but is placed here because of the proximity and available space. When at Minnesota University I worked with Dad, as a deckhand on this oil tanker during summer vacations, earning more there than I could in the Student Union Food Service, which was my only other possibility for employment.

V-mail form
August 10, 1943
Dear Dad,

I have been trying to get a letter off to you for some time now, but never seemed to find the time. It is now after 11 PM and the work has slowed down enough so that I can take a few minutes out.

Thanks so much for the letters you have been writing me – I enjoy them very much. I am glad to see that you went up for the extra license and made it. Did that include any extra tonnage or is it still only for the 1500 tons you had before? Do you think that Polings will do any better by you with the extra license? I don't suppose so but perhaps they will. I can hardly believe that Lannigan was too scared to make those trips with you. Why is he working on those ships, if he doesn't want to make those trips? He should have been on that day last January when we went up the Sound (I think it was to Stamford) when there was a 30 mile an hour gale and the temperature was about 10 below. That was some trip. The bow and port side got so caked up with ice we were listing way over, and we were wondering if we were going to make it or not. So Andy is still with you. His deferment was to be up in August – did he get another one? I suppose he did. Hear you had to use the deckhands for cooks. Have you got a new one?

Our food has improved very much lately – we have been getting fresh meat and vegetables, fruit, butter, etc., and it tastes good for a change.

Getting down toward the end of the sheet – better quite now with all my love to you, Mom, and Violet. Will try to write again soon.

Love, Arne

Lannigan and Andy were persons working on 'POLING BROTHERS # 3', the oil tanker Dad was captain of. The former was supposed to be a 'mate'—second in command, the second was a deckhand. For Lannigan to refuse a trip was inexcusable, as it resulted in much more work for Dad.

Tunisia, North Africa
August 14, 1943

Dear Mom,

I've been trying to get a letter off to you for the past four days but have been very busy. Just finished up a lot of stuff a few minutes ago – it is now 8:30 PM – and our day begins at 7:30 AM. There will probably be a bit more work in later, but will finish this letter first. As usual, there isn't much news – things are still pretty much the same.

Today, Smitty and I went swimming again – for about an hour – that's all the time we could spare. At least we got some sun and exercise – which I really need. Being in the office all day, I don't get much of a workout.

Oh yes, one thing I wanted to tell you – your letters are not censored. No one reads them but myself. I thought I had told you that once before – but maybe I hadn't. Anyway, you don't have to write English on that account – if you find it easier to write Norwegian, why go ahead, I will be able to understand it.

Yes, I had a letter from Roy – hope I can get time to write him soon. If he drops around to visit you – give him my greetings and tell him he will have a letter on the way pretty soon. Anna writes some very interesting letters, hope I hear from her again soon. I wonder why it is taking them so long to get Aleck started in Navigators' school. There's another letter I should write – to Aleck.

We are finally getting a permanent chaplain at our base.

When he comes, we will have regular church services – better recreation facilities, a library, *(as you can see, we did get a library)* and probably movies once in a while. Everybody is very anxious to see him come.

The base library

There are a few things I would like to have you send me, Mom, in particular, a bottle of Schaeffer's "Skrip" V-Black ink, and 2 or 3 black ties. If you get over to Macy's, go up to the uniform shop and ask them for enough quarter-inch gold braid (for lieutenant junior grade) for two suits of blues, and also two sets of silver collar bars, also for the same rank. This is so that if I get a promotion overseas, I will have that stuff on hand. I don't expect to be promoted until the first of the year, but don't tell them that. Just say, I expect a promotion soon. There isn't much else I can think of, except that I don't think my stationary will last very long, and if any more film is available (the same size and kind as last time) I can use some of that.

Well, it is getting late – the days are going by fast, and every day that goes by brings me closer to home. Must close for now.

Good night & pleasant dreams – and all my love to the best family.

Arne

P.S. Also ask uniform shop for one pair of lieut. (j.g.) shoulder boards. You can take all this out of the money I've sent you. In another 2 weeks, will send you some more money.

The promotion did come but not as soon as I hoped. However, the sleeve gold braid arrived from Mom and I was able to get it applied quite quickly. Regarding the bit about writing to me in Norwegian; mother only completed the 3rd grade before having to stop formal schooling in order to be more of a helper on the family farm. She never stopped learning, by reading everything she could lay her hands on. She learned English by requiring my brother Aleck and me to speak only English when we came home from school in the P.S. 170 grade school in Bay Ridge Brooklyn.

Tunisia, North Africa
Aug. 21, 1943

Dear Mom & Dad & Violet,

I have a few minutes now – so I will write a little letter. Haven't had much mail lately – had one from you 3 days ago – thanks so much. Had a letter from Aleck today – written June 30th addressed to my first station – also a card from Alma. Aleck said he had seen George Lund a few times in Texas again – and expected to see him some more. He sounded a little sad about being washed out of flying school, but sounded a lot more cheerful than he did in his previous letter.

It was nice to hear that George visited with you – I wish I could have been there to see him too. How did he like the idea of being an instructor? Too bad his folks weren't home. I like to hear Roy and Anna came over to visit you – sure wish I could have been with all of you. Hope they visit you often.

It is very warm today – must be around 100° - and a little sticky too. We expect rain very soon – perhaps that may cool things off – when it does rain.

The news seems to get better & better every day – perhaps we will see the end of this frightful war pretty soon. I hope so anyway. Perhaps we may see the end of German resistance by the year's end, but that may be asking too much.

The days are getting shorter – it gets dark around 8:30 PM now whereas a couple weeks ago, it was daylight until 9:30. Time really seems to fly. Here is a little poem written about the place I would like to be at now.

Home

These humble walls contain the essence of a home.
One need not ascertain or delve into a tome
To see a Mother's care imprinted on the place.
Each curtain, picture, chair, the candlesticks and vase,
Bespeak the loving touch accorded all these things,
By Mother's hand – all such for us contentment brings.

Must write Aleck a letter now. Keep smiling!
All my love, Arne

65

Tunisia, North Africa
August 30, 1943

Dear Mom,

Just a few lines to let you know I am feeling fine and in the best of health. There isn't much to write about, but will try to give you a little news anyway. Haven't had any mail from you for about two weeks now – I imagine it will all start coming in pretty soon.

Today, orders were issued that a certain number of men and officers would be required to take a ten mile hike each day. My turn comes tomorrow and then in another week I go again. I suppose that it to keep us in good condition. Well, I can use it for in my present job I don't get very much exercise. After playing baseball a couple of nights ago, my legs were very stiff and I could hardly move the next day. This hiking business should harden us up pretty good.

A few nights ago, some of our *(enlisted)* men arranged a little dinner party for the officers of our department. It was held in a little French restaurant by the seashore. Those boys really went to a lot of trouble to make the dinner a big success – they got some flour and coffee from our galley so the French woman could bake us a cake and have coffee – they decorated the table with flowers, and brought candles – it was wonderful. The lady did the serving, while her husband did most of the cooking. First we had anchovies with tomatoes, onions, & green peppers & spiced beets. Then we had an omelette made with spam and onions – mmmm – wonderful. Then came spaghetti with sauce, followed by steak and French fried potatoes. By that time we were getting kind of full, but the food kept coming. After the steak, we had a slice of melon, chocolate cake, grapes, and coffee. Don't you think that was a good meal? I was never so full after finishing – oh me oh my, but I couldn't stop eating cause it was so good.

The weather is getting much more pleasant now. It has cooled down considerable and the nights are a little chilly sometimes. We saw our first clouds in a couple of months a few days ago, and they were so pretty. I think we will have the start of the rainy season pretty soon and then it may not be so pleasant anymore.

Tomorrow is payday and in a few days I will send you either $150 or 200 dollars. That will be the last money orders I will send. My allotments will be taken out starting in September. One advantage to being over here is that I am saving a lot of money which will stand me in good stead when I get back. Have you received my other money orders yet? I sent a total of 400 dollars the end of July and the first part of August and I haven't heard whether you received any of it yet or not. Please let me know.

Must get back to work now. Will write again soon.

All my love,
Arne

V-mail form

September 1, 1943

Dear Dad,

This is more or less in the line of a birthday greeting for you. *(Dad's 58th birthday was the tenth).* I'm afraid a regular air-mail letter would not reach you in time, but I've been told these V-mail letters get there in about a week. Everything here is fine – weather perfect, cooling off pleasantly. A group of men and officers went on a ten mile hike this morning, and I went along. The purpose of these hikes is to condition us – but to coin a word, I think perhaps they will "uncondition" us. My feet were quite sore when I came back, but my legs were not tired. Maybe if I had used a different pair of shoes it would have been better. The captain and I were setting the pace – and we were really stepping out. We did the ten miles in 2 ½ hours.

I was paid today, and evidently they started taking out my $100 allotment in August, so mother should have a check by the time you get this. Please let me know if it came through – if it didn't, I can check up. The bonds won't start coming until the end of this month.

Well, Dad, here's hoping you have a very Happy Birthday and also that I'll be back to celebrate your next one. And much love to Mom & Violet.

Love from your son,
Arne

V-mail form
September 2, 1943
Dear Mom,

This is just a few lines to let you know that I got your package and 4 letters – after waiting over two weeks to hear from you. The package was swell, thanks so much. I now have enough candy to last me for quite a while. It was a long wait to get your letters – but I knew they would finally come. It is rather peculiar that you should be getting my mail regularly, and that your mail should not come in the same way. Well, as long as it does come thru after a while, that is enough. As you say, patience is a virtue.

We heard the great news that Italy surrendered last night* and we are very happy about it, of course. However, it doesn't mean that the end of the war is at hand – we are just that much closer to final victory – God speed the day. There will be more good news, but we still have a fight on our hands – and we can't say that we are thru until both Germany and Japan are out of the running. And that may not be such an easy task.

I also received Violet's letter today – and was very pleased to get it. She writes an interesting letter for a girl of her age. I will write her a letter very soon. It was nice to hear that George and Pete visited you – they are a nice pair of fellows – and I am also glad that Roy visits with you often. I suppose he must be quite busy going to school – but if you would, drop a little hint to him to write me again. I wrote him a letter some time ago but haven't heard from him since that letter you forwarded for him.

Have a physical exam tomorrow – better I get some sleep. Will write again soon.

Love to all,
Arne

*Of course, that reference was to the surrender of the Mussolini government - or possibly to the surrender of Sicily. Ahead of us were still the invasions of Salerno and Anzio and the long slogging fight up the boot of Italy, fighting mainly the Germans and those Italian troops who remained loyal to the Fascist regime.

Dear Mom,

It is very surprising to me that I haven't received any mail from you since Aug. 18, and none that I have received were dated later than July 30. Now I know you are writing, but it still seems kinda strange, because some of the fellows have gotten regular air-mail letters sent from home as late as Aug. 26. Well, one of these days I ought to get a whole stack of them at once.

I am including a money order for $77.50 – didn't have enough to make an even 100 dollars. Put $50 in the bank for me, and keep the $27.50 for your self – another payment on my debt to you. I looked over my books just now, and including this money order, I have repaid you $450 and saved $500 for myself. That's pretty good, I think, and before we know it, it will be twice that much.

I had another letter from Aleck yesterday, the third in about 2 weeks. It's swell to hear from him – and he sounds much more cheerful now than he ever did. I think the Navigators' course is much easier than the pilot training – at least it seems that way. He seems to have more time to live. He also said that soon he might fly up to Minneapolis – so I wrote and asked him if he wouldn't call up Virginia – it would be nice if they could meet.

Nothing of importance that's new. We have a chaplain on the base finally – we won't have to travel to go to church anymore. He held his first services yesterday, and seems like a nice fellow. He comes from the South and is an Episcopalian.

I had a shot in the arm today – a typhus booster. My arm is a little sore but not stiff. I am due for another one in a month. You see, every six months it is required that you get these shots to keep up your immunity to various diseases.

Well Mom, I am going down to the post office now to see if I have any mail from you – here's hoping. Love to Dad on his birthday & also to Violet a kiss & hug.

Your loving son,

Arne

V-mail form
September 14, 1943
Dear Mom & Dad,

A few days ago there was a sudden spurt of mail and I received quite a bit from you. I even received a letter from Violet, one from Dad, and one from Aleck. And of course, I had a few from my friends from the West. It was swell to hear from everybody – especially after such a long time without hearing. Most of the mail was about a month old – nothing later than the 15th of August. Yet it was all very welcome. Now I suppose there will be another period of two weeks or so before I get anymore – hope not. Thanks again for the package and the film. Sunday, we went out and I took quite a few pictures which should be pretty good if they turn out. Will send you some as soon as I get them back again.

The heat is still with us, though it is much cooler in the evenings and it is wonderful to sleep at night – I have to use one blanket now, when a few weeks ago, I just slept in my pajamas with nothing else. The days are just as warm as they were a month ago, and that was too hot to suit me – guess I thrive in colder climates. I imagine that we will have the rainy season with us pretty soon – next month anyway. That will be some experience – I understand that it rains steadily all day for days and weeks at a time. Well, I have a good raincoat, boots, and cap so I am all fixed for that when it comes.

We haven't been so busy lately – and we are not too sorry at that. It is good to get a little time for relaxation once in awhile. Today, I was up on the roof doing a little laundry, but it is a discouraging job for without hot water it is impossible to get things clean. And there is no way around here that you can heat water in sufficient quantities to do the right kind of a job either. Guess I will send it all out next time, even though the local French people don't do such a very good job either – and are expensive and how!!

Tomorrow is payday – and I have $30 coming – the rest you should be getting in allotments. *(A freshly minted Ensign received pay of $130 per month plus $30 meal allowance)* I won't draw any of it because I still have about $50 in cash on me and that is more than enough to last the rest of the month and longer. Mother, I wish you would continue to take half of the $100 allotment, instead of putting it all in the bank for me like you wrote

71

of once. It will make me feel better, and you can always use it later if you haven't any use for it now. Put it away for a house if you have no other plans for it. Wish it was more I could give you, but I would like to have some to go on when I get out.

I would like to go back to school again for my Masters Degree – have I told you about those plans of mine? When there is more time and space, will tell you about it.

Time for supper now – will close for the time being.
Love & kisses to all,

Arne

V-mail form
September 17, 1943
Dear Dad,

It was swell to get your letter of August 22 – thanks for writing me. This letter, of necessity, must be rather short, for I have the midnight duty, and there is still some work to be done.

Sorry to hear that you have to work so hard – I realize that doing the work of two is not so easy – and if I were you, I wouldn't work too hard – I don't think it is worth it. Even though you get extra money for it, it is not so good because at your age, you should be able to relax and enjoy life. Poling (*Poling Brothers is the company Pop worked for*) should be able to fix up something so that you wouldn't have to be going night and day – I don't blame Andy for trying to get something better, but it really did leave you in sort of a hole, didn't it?

Last Sunday, we took a little trip around the countryside and saw some very interesting sights. One place was the site of the ancient temple of Baal and Tanit, the gods that we read about in the Bible. The people in those days used to sacrifice little babies by throwing them into the mouth of an idol in which there was a raging fire. At this place, we saw the small earthen jugs that were used to hold the cremated remains of these babies and the little gravestones that were used to mark the place of burial. The stones had some very interesting inscriptions on them. Then we went to another place where there was a water reservoir over two thousand years old – and still in use. There are so many places of interest over here – I've got some pictures of them and will send them as soon as possible. Not much more room. Good night and love to all,

Arne

The picture on this page is of G.B. Long, head of my division, inside a cave where the urns of cremated babies' ashes were located.

73

V-mail form
September 26, 1943
Dear Mom,

Today I received your letter of August 25th – did I tell you that about five days ago I received five letters, pardon me, it was four, from you? It really is nice to hear from home – reading your letters makes me think I am in Bay Ridge for a few minutes, in the back yard – sitting in a deck chair, or in the living room listening to the radio, or in the kitchen eating some of your wonderful apple pie, or some little thing like that. Maybe it won't be too long before such a time will be possible – although I don't mean to get your hopes up, for there are no indications that we will be sent home yet.

It is getting dark earlier and earlier every evening now – and last night we put our clocks back an hour and that made it dark at seven this evening. It looked very much like rain this afternoon, and I wouldn't be surprised if we had a few good downpours soon. I imagine that it is really getting to be the autumn weather at home now – with coats and jackets being worn. Well, during the daytime, we are still going without anything more than a shirt – and still feel warm. The nights are getting cooler and cooler though, and a blanket is a definite necessity now.

We had church services today – Chaplain Gray gave a good sermon. My friend Mike Silseth, the chaplain from the first base I was at, was down here a few days ago for a visit – it was nice to see him again. He didn't have much to say – guess things are pretty quiet where he is now. 'Course he is still a little homesick for his wife and I don't blame him. I suppose church at home has started in full swing again, with Pastor Okdale back. Are there any new faces there, or are there less than there used to be?

We had steak and ice cream for dinner today – that steak was really swell, and the vanilla ice cream – mmmmm! There evidently is no more fresh butter left for we are getting the "treated butter" again – that is, butter that has been fixed up so that it won't melt in temperatures up to 100 degrees. After the fresh variety, it doesn't taste so good for it won't melt in your mouth, and feels like wax. However, we shouldn't complain for there are many peoples who haven't even that, and would be very happy to get that.

I saw a movie last night, and in a news reel, saw some of the fighting that went on just a few miles from here in the latter

74

part of April. Was a rather peculiar feeling. Then it also showed a scene of Times Square in New York, and it was the nicest sight I had seen in a long time – for it was a bit of home – one of the fellows sitting nearby said he wished he could walk right thru the screen then, and on to Broadway – I thought so too.

Looks like I must close – my love and kisses to you all at home,

Arne

Tunisia, N. Africa
Sept. 27, 1943

Dear Mom,

Here it is – a whole week since I last wrote you – or did I drop you a V-mail last week sometime? Anyway, I've received quite a bit of mail lately, and have been rather hard put to answer them all – letters have come in from almost everyone that has ever written me before – and let me tell you it's really wonderful to receive it too!

Today I took a ride in a jeep on business – guess we must have traveled at least 80 to 100 miles. The country here is so different from the U.S. There are very few trees, the hills are barren and rough, the farms look scraggly and uncared for, and most everything looks kinda run-down. Of course, there are many amazing landmarks and historic sites to see, some of which I've already told you about. Today, we saw the ruins of the ancient aqueduct (Violet can tell you what that is). It was built by the Romans over two thousand years ago to bring water from a reservoir 30 miles or more away, into their city. It is remarkably well preserved, and it is a tribute to the engineering skill of those ancient peoples.

Had a letter from Dad today – will try to answer it tomorrow or the next day. I'm glad to hear you received all my money orders, and that the government check is coming thru all right. Someday, that money will be of great use – and this is the time to save it – don't you think?

How do you get along with the point rationing? Is there any shortage of foods – or are you getting enough to eat?

It is quite late – must close now – with a wish for "Pleasant Dreams" – and Love to you all,

Arne

V-mail form

October 3, 1943

Dear Mother,

I received your "V" mail letter of Sept. 17 today – thank you so much. I finally have been receiving some of your mail – maybe most of what you have sent. There may be a few letters yet missing. They will probably show up soon. So you have finally received all the money I sent you. Well, that is one thing off my mind. The 877.50 plus the 25 dollars I sent as a present is correct. From now on, you will be getting the money as allotment checks – that will be a little better. The bond should start coming the beginning of October – you probably have received the first one already – let me know when you get it.

I certainly am glad that you are getting my letters regularly – I wish I could write more often, but that is oftentimes rather difficult to do. I try to write once a week anyway, and if possible get two off. The V mail letter I received from you today seemed to come pretty fast – at least it took less time than some of the other letters I have gotten from you. Write a few more – from what I have been able to gather, they seem to take about the same length of time as the regular mail.

Went to church again today – the chaplain gave a very interesting sermon. He spoke of the symbolism of the fish in the Christian faith. Some time it may be interesting for you to ask Pastor Okdale to tell you about the meaning of the fish symbol – and the acrostic that the Greek for fish spells out. The word in Greek is ichthus. If he can't tell you – I will tell you about it.

The weather here is very pleasant now – it has cooled off enough so that we can wear ties in the daytime, and sometimes jackets too. At night, I use two blankets now, and the coolness is just perfect for sleeping. We have had a few showers already, and I suspect that there are more on the way. Yes, the rainy season is almost here, and am I glad that I have good rain clothes, hat, coat, and boots. I bought a blue flannel shirt not so long ago, which will be nice and warm for the cool winter days here. I also bought some more underwear, six undershirts and six shorts, so please don't send me any more clothes. I have plenty to last for a number of years now.

I took a few more pictures today, and turned them in and another roll that I spoke of last time, so perhaps the next time I write I will

Photo taken with filter

be able to send you a few. There were the most beautiful clouds in the sky today, and with my red filter for the camera, I should have some good pictures. (*This photo is one with the red filter. It is a black and white photo and I wish it was in color*).

Everything is much the same here – the doctor says he thinks I have gained some weight – hope he is right. I feel fine anyway, and I hope all at home feel the same. Think I better say goodnight for now. It is quite late and I must be up early in the morning.

Love to you all,

Arne

Ancient Roman Columns

Temple of Jupiter

V-mail form
October 19, 1943
Dearest Mother,

Today I received two v-mail letters from you – dated Oct. 3 and 8. A few days ago, I received another letter from you regular mail, dated Sept. 15th. I hope you are writing a few regular mail letters in between the v-mail, because although the v-mail does seem to come through much quicker, they haven't much room on them and you can't say very much.

I know I should write to you more often – I know what it is to sit and wait for mail and then find out there is none for you, but there is so little to write about – we go through the same routine every day – nothing new ever seems to happen, and I don't like to say the same things over and over – which is exactly what I am doing now.

Mother, it sounds to me like you are not quite following my instructions in regards to the money I have been sending home. According to my books, I should have saved $550 dollars minus the bills which you have been paying for me – those bills totaling about one hundred dollars, which should leave about 450 dollars in my bank account. And if you had been taking your fifty dollars out of the hundred every time, I should have repaid you exactly five hundred dollars. In the future, Mom, please take your half and put in the bank, or use it in any way you want, but pay my bills and insurance out of my half and put the rest of what's left in my account. I appreciate your wanting my savings to grow, but I also want to square away all my debts, so that when I come back, I will be able to start off with a clean slate.

I am glad to hear my bonds are starting to come through – did your idea of getting a safe deposit box for them and your own ever materialize? That reminds me – I have been looking around here for some Christmas presents to send home – but the selection is very limited. In fact there is just about nothing worthwhile, so I am going to send you and Dad some money, and you can buy something for yourself or get some bonds – whichever you choose to do. I am sending a small thing to Violet, and Aleck is also going to be taken care of. It is swell of you to send me a Christmas package, but you shouldn't send more than one – that would be plenty for me.

Yes, I also wish we had bought that house down 71st Street. * It really was a nice place and such a good location. You ought to keep your eyes open, perhaps it will be for sale again, or some other house like it around the same neighborhood – never can tell. I hope Dad isn't working too hard – I don't suppose he has a new mate yet. Wish I were there to give him a hand. I have not heard from Aleck for some time now – wish he'd write soon. I am feeling fine here, and hope Violet is feeling better now.
Love to you all from,

Your loving son,
Arne

This was a beautiful one- family house near Shore Road, in a very lovely neighborhood. This was in the early 40s. The seller wanted $5,200 but my mother refused to go higher than $5,000, so her offer was refused. It was sold to another buyer, who made a big profit when several years later many homes in the neighborhood, including this one, were bought up, the houses razed and a large apartment building replaced them all. It really gave me pangs when I heard the later news, thinking that the folks could have done very well if they had been willing to raise the offer to the sellers' best price. But that is always "Monday Morning Quarterbacking".

V-mail form
October 27, 1943
Dear Mother,

Just a short note to let you know everything is fine – but no mail from you or anyone else. It is almost two weeks now since I've heard from you, but then I can't complain too much for almost everyone else has been in the same situation. Well, there is always tomorrow to look forward to.

We had another dinner at the little French restaurant by the seashore a few nights ago – and it was excellent. To start off with, we had chilled grapefruit juice, then a barley soup, followed by a salad consisting of green peppers, tomatoes, sardines covered by a fine salad dressing. Then there was a steak with mixed vegetables for the main course, and was it good! The dessert was a special type of omelette made with a rum sauce which was something really super-duper. There was also a bowl of fresh dates and of course with the main courses there was a dark sour bread which was also good. These French people are good cooks, there's no question about it.

It has started to get much cooler nowadays – I have already added a third blanket for my bed, a few nights ago I woke up and found myself shivering a bit. And of course, during the day, we wear jackets or sweaters. There has been some rain lately too, and more is expected very soon. It is a nice change but I hope we get our heating units soon. You see, in these buildings there are no furnaces or provisions for them, so the Navy has ordered space heaters to put in the various rooms. That should solve the problem.

I told you, didn't I, that the package from Macy's arrived, and now I am all set. I don't imagine it will be necessary to use that stuff until after the first of the year sometime, but it is good to be prepared for any contingency. I hope you aren't going to any trouble to send anything for Christmas, for I have just about everything I need.

Day before yesterday, our department got a new chief petty officer. He is a chief radioman, and his name is Jensen also. Was I surprised! All the fellows thought there may be a little difficulty in telling us apart – what do you think about that?

How is Aleck doing? I haven't heard from him or about him for a long time. I suppose his course of instruction at navigator's school is pretty near over, isn't it? And what do you hear from your "other boys" – George, Pete, Roy, and all the rest?

I see my space is growing short, as it always does much too soon – I'll try to write soon again. In the meantime, much love to Violet, Dad and of course to yourself from---------Your loving son,

Arne

Tunisia, North Africa
November 4, 1943
Dear Dad,

It's been better than two weeks now since I had any mail – but I suppose I can't kick, for the other men haven't been getting any either. Yet it is a little disheartening not to get any news from home.

I did get Mother's package yesterday – the one with the tie, ink, stationery, film, candy, and ointment – and it was swell. Thanks so very much. You shouldn't send any more though – I have enough candy & cigarettes to start a store of my own, and I have everything else I need, and what I need I can buy at our ship's store.

The other day I had to make a business trip to a nearby base *(most likely Bizerte)* about 60 miles away, and had a good time driving a jeep through the countryside. The scenery is very striking and at times beautiful. On the way back, we picked up an Army sergeant who was a gunner on a bomber. He had just completed his 50th mission and was going back to the States for awhile. He had seen a lot of action and some of the stories he told would curl your hair. Lately, he had been based in Italy, and what he tells of that land is shocking. He said that some of the cities he had seen were completely leveled – hardly one brick left on another. The people over there are starving – he said at night women & children would come around the Army encampments to pick up scraps thrown away by our soldiers. Of course, our boys gave some of their own away, but that wasn't enough. And before the Germans left positions they had held, they did everything possible to sabotage. They threw salt, drugs, and anything else into wells & water supplies, and took with them anything of value – all scraps of food the civilians had – and what they couldn't take along, they destroyed. It's hard to believe anyone human could do such things. I certainly hope this war will soon end – so that all these terrible things will cease.

There isn't much news from here, everything is just about the same – I'm feeling fine, we're getting good food, and all is well. Give my love to Mom & Violet!

Love from your son,
Arne

84

Tunisia, North Africa
November 8, 1943
Dear Mom,

At last we are starting to get a little mail. I received your package a few days ago – think I mentioned it in the letter I wrote Pop. Thanks again for everything. Three days ago I also had two letters from you, one a V-mail dated Oct 18, and the other an air-mail dated Aug 29!!! Can you imagine that? – an air-mail letter taking more than two months to reach me? And some of them have arrived in 6-7 days.

The rainy season seems to have come to stay – it has been drizzling for the last couple of days. It has also become somewhat colder – and I've caught a little cold. It isn't anything to worry about, and should be gone pretty soon. It's a good thing I have Aleck's sweater with me – it's nice and warm, and although it isn't strictly correct uniform wear, I'm still going to wear it.

I see Roy is still in New York – but he still hasn't written to me – and I haven't heard from Anna since September. If you see them again, please tell them I'm expecting to hear from them. And how is Aleck doing? Haven't heard from him for a long time.

In your old letter I got all the figures on my finances & bank account. Mother, in regard to the money in my bank account, I want you to promise me that you will withdraw $100 out of my account and put it in your own. In looking through my records and comparing them with the figures you sent, I see that two of those $100 money orders you did not take your $50 share. Therefore you are $100 behind what you should have received. When you take that $100 (and it is not a Christmas present, but a repayment) and add it to your bank account, I will have repaid you $550 since the first of the year up to and including the allotment check you should have received the 2nd or 3rd of Nov. (That includes the bonds, the cash I gave you in February, and the money orders I've sent, and the allotment check.) And as of the same time (first part of Nov.) after you've taken out the $100, there should be $530 minus the insurance for October (and any other bills) in my bank account. Please promise you will do this, Mom.

It is getting late, and I should get some rest – so I'll say
Good-night & God bless you all,

All my love, Arne

Tunisia, North Africa
November 15, 1943
Dear Mom,

At last we had some mail – a letter each from you and Pop – and a few more. Thanks for your letters – they mean so much.

I have been made official base photographer by our new captain, and I think it is going to be a lot of fun. Already he has given me a couple of jobs in that line. Our Executive Officer had a camera which didn't work so well, and asked me to look it over. I think it is in pretty good shape now, but it still has to be tested. He thought that was great.

Did I tell you I had an unlucky break and lost one of the lenses to my glasses? Well, tomorrow I have to make a trip to an Army hospital for an examination so I can get a new pair. I can get along without them as far as seeing is concerned, but my eyes get tired quickly without them because I am doing a lot of close work – writing, reading, etc. If the Army can't get me a pair, I'll have to send to Minneapolis for a copy of the old ones.

Mother, today is payday, and when I get my money, I will send you an order for $25 as a Christmas present. With it you can buy yourself and Pop something you would like. There is nothing at all to buy here that would be worthwhile, and that's the only way I can think of to give you something. I am sending Violet a small thing – I don't think it's much, but perhaps when I get back-!

There are no Christmas cards to be had here, so I am making some – probably this letter will get to you around Christmas time, and if it does, remember I am with you all in spirit, and maybe next year I shall be there in person. A very Joyous Holiday Season to all, and May the New Year see Victory & Peace.

Love to you all,
Arne

Mr. & Mrs. Karl G. Jensen
825 - 70 Street
Brooklyn, New York
New York

Ens A. Jensen, USNR
Navy 74 % Fleet P.O.
New York N.Y.
November 14, 1945

Christmas Greetings

Our Eyes Are In The East
But Our Hearts Are In The West

Don't forget - I am
with you in my heart
all my love,
Ole

85th DRS

Miss Violet Jensen
823 70 Street
Brooklyn, N.Y.
New York

Ens A. Jensen USNR
Navy 141, c/o F.P.O.
New York, N.Y.
November 16, 1943

MERRY CHRISTMAS
NORTH AFRICA 1943

and a Happy New Year '44!

Tunisia, North Africa
November 23, 1943

Dear Mother & Dad & Violet,

 I'm behind in my letter writing – but I have been very busy during the past week. You see, I have been made official base photographer in addition to my other duties and the skipper gave me a lot of work to do. First I had to get the darkroom fixed up – then I had to take pictures of the inspection of personnel last Saturday – develop the film & make prints, and a few other jobs in that line. But it's lots of fun and good experience. The Captain likes my work – for I made some good pictures. Hope I don't run out of film too soon.

Here is a copy of my official appointment letter.

ADVANCED AMPHIBIOUS
TRAINING BASE, NAVY #94 FPO   (haf)
NEW YORK, NEW YORK.

22 November 1943.

TO WHOM IT MAY CONCERN:

 1. As of this date Ensign A. JENSEN, USNR, has been designated official photographer for this base.

 2. Any assistance which can be rendered him in the execution of his duties will be greatly appreciated.

John B. Baltzer

JOHN B. BALTZER,
Lieutenant, USNR.,
Executive Officer.

You speak of there being plenty of meat now at home – well, we have been having wonderful food lately – roasts, chicken, hams, and a few days ago we got our turkeys for Thanksgiving and

Christmas. We have fresh apples & oranges, and our supply officer is going to get frozen strawberries & peaches today.

This morning we had fresh scrambled eggs. Bet you won't recognize me when I get back – I'll be so fat. Yep, we have it pretty nice all right.

I am including a few pictures for you – the one of me isn't so good, but it shows that I've gained some weight – if nothing else. The other two were taken in this vicinity in the evening so they are a little on the dark side.

I am glad to hear that Roy & Anna are engaged. Perhaps Anna will supplement Roy's more impulsive nature, and add the balance which will make him the great success he is capable of being. If anyone can do it, she can.

It seems that almost every time you write, you tell of someone either becoming engaged or getting married. By golly, almost all the kids at Bethany are now in that condition. Well, more power to them.

Well, folks, I'll be thinking of you tomorrow when I eat my Thanksgiving turkey – hope you have one too. Bye for now!

All my love, Arne

One of my first assignments as Official Base Photographer was to record the 'Captains Inspection'. The following pages show some of the shots taken.

Captain's Inspection

Captain ready to inspect.

Captain starting rounds

Base Officers

Base enlisted men

'Sea Bee' Platoon

Captain & CB Lieutenant

Captain about to give dismissal orders. Notice dog.

Tunisia, North Africa
November 30, 1943

Dear Mom & Dad & Violet,

Here it is a whole week since I last wrote – I had good intentions of writing oftener, but I've been given a couple of extra jobs which take up quite a bit of time. In addition to my regular duties in the Communications division, the captain made me official photographer for the base (*see previous letter)* and also made me the mess treasurer. Before I forget it, would you see if you could get me one or two rolls of Kodacolor film (size 120 or 620)? I might be able to get some beautiful pictures with those.

Just a few minutes before starting this letter, Ed and I just came from the dark room where we had developed 4 rolls (one of mine). It is such an interesting job, and I get a lot of fun out of it. We have made many pictures already, and I am including some snaps of the captain's inspection about a week ago *(see preceding page)* - then you can see what a fine bunch of men we have here. I hope to be able to send you more from now on.

Last Thursday we had our Thanksgiving dinner, and very good it was too. We had turkey, of course, mashed potatoes, giblet gravy, green peas, bread & butter, chocolate cake, and coffee. There were flowers on the table, and some of the boys had made up some small menu folders with a turkey drawn in, and then lettered across the front was printed "Thanksgiving Day-1943". Yes, it was very nice. The chaplain had a service that morning, and almost everyone was there.

Two views of our Thanksgiving dining tables

On Sunday we climbed the big mountain across the bay again – and I think I got some good pictures of it. It was good exercise, and we had a good time. (*The mountain is called Bou Kornin.*)

Panorama taken from top of Bou Kornin
(*The picture above is a panorama with 3 images pasted together, taken from the mountain top*) We also visited a French museum which had some mosaics (pictures made with different colored, small stone tiles set in cement) of the early Christian days – and real old statues, and so many other things.

So far I've received 3 Christmas packages from you, the last one came today. One came two days ago, and the other one the day before that. Thanks so very much!! We will have a pretty good Christmas even though we will be away from home. Oh yes, I got one package from Mildred Olson – from the church I guess – it was candy. I have so much candy and toilet articles now, I won't have to buy any for a long time. Then I got a package from Jean Anne, and from Virginia I got one – she says she sent two, so there is another on the way. The mail has been very good lately – have had quite a number of letters from you, and finally got one from Aleck yesterday. Yes, we are very well off here – no complaints, except that we aren't home.

Well, I must go to bed now – Merry Christmas to you all – and all my love,

Arne

P.S. Thank Tante Inga & Uncle Paul for the Christmas presents they sent me! Oh yes, I did get the pictures you sent me – thanks so much!

Tunisia, North Africa
Dec 4th, 1943

Dear Dad,

This evening is almost gone, and soon I will go to bed, but first I wanted to write you a few lines. The news was just on the radio – and it sound very good – just hope it gets so much better so that in a short while we will hear that the war is over!

This morning the captain held an inspection of our sleeping quarters, and working area – he was very much pleased with our division, because it was so clean and neat.

I weighed myself the other day, first time since February, and by golly, I weighed 7 pounds more than when I left. We have had such good food, I would have been surprised if I had not gained a bit. We have started an exercise class too – and that will help keep us in trim.

This week I have the night duty, so if any important messages come in, I have to get up to take care of them. But it isn't so bad.

Last night we had a stage show put on by a group of soldiers. They were very good – kept us laughing for 2 hours. There were comedians, jugglers, acrobats, singers; they had a fine orchestra, a hill-billy band, and so much other talent. It was a pleasure to watch them. One of them imitated Hitler giving a speech, and we just about fell off our chairs laughing. We've had some good shows, but this was the best one.

Dad, I hope you don't work too hard, especially now during the winter when it's so much harder. And I hope you have a good cook – that helps a lot. Wish I were there to help you.

I want to thank all of you for all the packages you sent. Even though I'll be away from home at Christmas, it won't be too bad with all those things to remember you all by, and things could be so much worse.

Gotta go to sleep now – keep your chin up and,
Love,
Arne

P.S. Love to Mother & Violet too

V-mail form
December 6, 1943
Dear Mom,

Here are a few lines to let you know that everything is fine with me, and I hope that I hear the same from you soon. I have had letters from almost everyone but you in the last week or so. 'Course, it may be that tomorrow I will get a whole stack of it from you, anyway I hope so.

Yesterday, I took a little trip about fifty miles inland from here and saw some very interesting things. There were some ruins that were very well preserved, among them the temple of the ancient Greek or Roman god Jupiter. There were only a few pillars left standing, and the

Temple of Jupiter

Ancient mosaic floor

mosaic floors, but if you strained your imagination, you could see an impressive structure with gleaming marble all around, fountains, and gardens, and beautiful homes. Now all that is left is a few pillars, and these mosaics with weeds growing up between the stones. We met an Army lieutenant along the way and he showed us all that and more too. A swell fellow, who was in the Air Corps as a bombardier. I thought it was pretty nice of him to show us around, and thought of Aleck. Some day he may be out at a place like this. We had some fried chicken along for our lunch, and of course we shared it with him. He thought it was wonderful to eat chicken again – he had been getting only "C" rations, with fresh meat only about once a month. You can imagine what a treat it was for him to get fried chicken then! I took some pictures on this trip, and today I developed them. They came out swell, and when they are printed up, I will send you some. Space is growing short, so I will close with love to Violet, and Dad, and to my favorite Mother!

Arne

97

V-mail form
December 12, 1943
Dear Mom,

My typing isn't so good tonight, but I thought I'd drop you a few lines to let you know that I got another package from you a few days ago – also two from Virginia and one from her aunt. I can't understand where you get all the candy from – we seem to have it all over here, but thanks so much – it means so much to us to get things from home. One of Virginia's packages had cookies, fudge, and a fruit cake in it – the other one I am saving for Christmas – it has a label marked, "do not open before Dec. 25" on it.

My days have been very busy lately, between my regular duties, and the darkroom, there hasn't been much time for letter writing. Hope to catch up soon, though and then it won't be so bad. So many of the boys want pictures to send home, and I know how much the pictures mean to the folks at home, so I try to help them out a little.

We had a good dinner today – fried chicken, mashed potatoes, peas, and fruit cocktail for dessert. I told you I think, that I weighed myself recently and found that I had gained about seven pounds since I left the States. Pretty good for me, isn't it? Well, perhaps I can gain a few more pounds before I get back home – especially on the good food we have been getting.

We have had a little rain lately, but not the amount we have been expecting. Seems funny, this is supposed to be a place where there is so much rain during the winter months, but it hasn't been worse than New York during a similar period. Today was a beautiful sunshiny day – and so I hung my blankets out to air. I should be able to sleep well tonight – so G'night and Love to all,
Arne

My Dearest Mother,

Tonight I had to write you a special letter – I shouldn't say had to – instead I'll say I want to, for today is your birthday. I don't remember how many years "young" you are, but what difference does age make? To me you will always be the same as I first remember you, back in Norway – a very special person, some one to go to when I fell and hurt my knee, someone to sew up the pants that I ripped climbing a tree, someone to whom I could go when I wanted "sviskesjeve med sukker paa" (*a slice of raisin bread with sugar on it*) and someone who would tuck me in at night, say my prayers with me, and give me a kiss that would send me off into dreamland. Yes, just the dearest and sweetest person a fellow could have for a mother. God was certainly kind to me when he chose my parents.

It will be kind of lonesome this Christmas not to be with you – but things could be so much worse. I'll wager we will have a very nice Christmas here – probably better food than you folks back home, and with all the packages I've received, it will be almost like home – except for not having those I love near me. I hope you won't be too lonesome, and that perhaps Aleck will be there. By this time he should be all done, and probably will be home for a good furlough or leave. He deserves it!

Yesterday, I received two letters from you – one a V-mail dated Nov 23. Yes, I did receive the pictures you sent – they were very nice, and I am enclosing some pictures for you – as a sort of birthday present. I have been very busy lately getting an enlarger built. *(This 'enlarger' used my camera as the optical system, with the negative to be enlarged placed at the image plane of the camera. A hooded light source sat above the camera, both on an adjustable height support, and the print paper is below the camera.)* Finally it is done, and today I made my first enlargements. They weren't perfect, but were pretty good anyway. I enjoy photography so much and get a big kick out of this job. The captain saw the enlargements, and he was very pleased with them too. Taps are being played, and I am rather sleepy – I will say good night now to the best Mother a fellow could have. Hope you had a very Happy Birthday – and here's wishing you many more!   All my love,   Arne

V-mail form
December 23, 1943
Dear Mom, Dad, and Violet,

Just another little v-mail to let you know I am thinking about you all and wishing that I could be with you. Today I got another letter from you, Mom, an air mail from Dec. 2nd. Thanks so much. It is almost impossible for me to keep up with all the letters I have been getting lately. In two days I received over 20 letters and cards. It was a wonderful feeling to get them all, but it would have been more fun to have them spread over a long period of time instead. But I'm not complaining – I'd rather have them come that way than not at all.

In the last few days I have been going steady about 17-18 hours a day. Besides my regular work, there have been so many other things to do in preparation for the Christmas holidays. Some

Roommate Dave Teske

of the boys went out and found some trees which we decorated and set up in the various parts of our building – one in our club room, one in the recreation hall, one in the sick bay, and one in the crew's clubroom. And then I had to find some stuff to decorate the mess hall with –

wasn't much, but gave it a little color. And then we made over two hundred pictures for the men – and then there were menu folders to make up for the Christmas dinner. I am a little tired, but it has been a lot of fun. It reminded me of the time Aleck and I stayed up most of Christmas Eve and that night to print up the Scribe for Christmas Day. *The Scribe was a newsletter put out by the Junior Luther League (kids 14 to 17) at Bethany Lutheran Church*

Well, here we are at the bottom of the sheet again, so I better say so long for now – God be with you all.

All my love,
Arne

100

Hi there Sis,

This may reach you a little late for your birthday – but thought I'd try to write you a little greeting anyway. I want to thank you for the very nice Christmas card and letter you sent me – they were appreciated no end, and it was really swell hearing from my favorite sister again.

We had a very nice Christmas here in Africa. Xmas Eve we had midnight services and communion – and I thought it was beautiful. I opened the rest of my Christmas packages after supper that evening, and boy, did I get a lot of nice gifts. All the things you and Mom and Dad sent were swell – I guess I could open a candy store of my own with just the candy alone. Virginia sent me a real nice leather wallet, a book of poetry, a little pocket picture album, a chess set (small) and a service prayer book. Her mother sent me a key case which matched the wallet, her aunt sent a leather correspondence folio, and her father sent me some cigarettes. Then I received a box of candy from Mildred Nelson, a tobacco pouch and a fruit cake from Jean Anne out in Minnesota – jeepers, Santa really took good care of me this year. How did he treat you?

Christmas day we had a wonderful turkey dinner – with all

the trimmings – I had that stuffed feeling for a day after that. Our tables were nicely decorated with green branches and candlesticks, and we had a Christmas tree all decorated up just like home!

Christmas dinner tables

I had a letter from Aleck just a few days ago, and of course, you know that he has a Lt. in front of his name on the return address now – and I think that is swell. He worked hard for it and deserves all the credit in the world.

101

I have been very busy with my photographic work lately, especially since my enlarger has been finished and put in operation. I have made some pretty good pictures – all in all, I have about 250 of them – hope that I can show them to you pretty soon. If not, they will always keep. Am sending a few along as samples. Hope you like them.

It has been raining quite a bit here lately, but we still have nice days – and it never gets very cold. The coldest day we have had was around 35 degrees and that is not even down to freezing – so you can see I don't need any winter clothes like I did in Minnesota. I miss the snow and ice though, kinda wish we had a little of that around here, but then you can't have everything.

Well, Violet, here's wishing you a very happy birthday, many returns of the day, and many more like them. Hope I can help you celebrate your next one. All my love to Mom and Dad.

Love from your big brother,
Arne

I must insert here a story I would never have written home about, and of which I am not very proud.

December 31, 1943

We had to have a New Year's Eve party, there on the 'Dark Continent', so at base time 2200 hours, we were all in the Officer's Club ready to celebrate. There was some bottled hard liquor and lots of different wines, and even some champagne. We all started off with a glass of wine and some nibbles. There were jokes told, and songs were sung, and at midnight, the champagne was uncorked and everyone toasted the New Year, and we sang "Old Lang Syne". After that the hard liquor was enjoyed to the last drop, and only the wines were left. I left the party at about 0200 hours, feeling quite 'woozy'.

On New Year's Day I awoke with a real 'hangover'! It was a splitting headache that lasted all day. I did remember having a good time the night before, but could not remember much about the time after midnight. That bothered me because of possible stupid things I may have said, but then I put that worry away because everyone was pretty much in the same boat. I believe the mixture of the different kinds of alcohol was the reason.

That was the first time I ever was so inebriated, and I promised myself I would not do that again. (The next time was decades later, but that is another story for a different book).

Before we start the 1944 letters I want to add several stories whose chronology escapes me, but since they are worthy of telling, here they are, in normal font style.

"Mother Perry's Kitchen"

One of our enlisted men had a passion for cooking, and quite

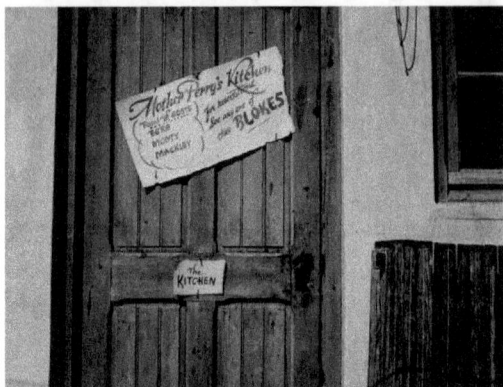

often entertained his fellow seamen with 'home-cooked' dinners. Like many ingenious service men, he had scrounged enough necessary kitchen ware to operate his private version.

Doorway to "Mother Perry's Kitchen"
The brightness and contrast were adjusted to make the sign more readable.

There came a time when the work load at the base had decreased significantly, so that Mother Perry and some of his friends offered to serve a dinner for the officers of the group they were a part of. We were duly invited and we obviously accepted.

When the day came, we gathered first in the dining room shown on the right and later moved to the roof of the building, where his kitchen was located.

It was a sumptuous meal and I wish I could remember what he cooked. He must have done some shopping in the Tunis markets, and quite possibly scrounged some stuff from the galley. When the meal was over, he got a loud round of applause and shouts of 'Well Done, Mother Perry!'

Feasting Officers

104

A Flight to Bizerte

At one time I was given the opportunity of flying in a Navy seaplane (a two-seater) with a pair of pilots who had a mission to deliver some documents to Bizerte. Of course I said YES! I sat in the back seat of one of the planes. I will add some photos of that memorable flight.

The companion seaplane

Looking out to the right

Coastline of Tunis area

Surface view on the way

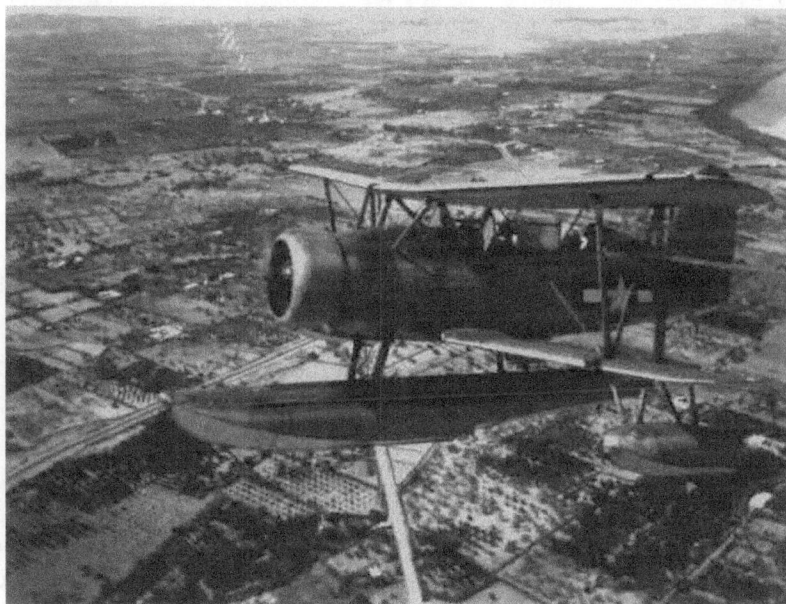

Companion over edge of Tunis

It was a real fun flight and I was so happy to have had it.

The Prune Alcohol Caper

There came a time when the Officer's Club bar ran out of branded liquor, and there were many empty bottles to prove it. This situation sent my clever roommate Dave Teske into the planning and execution of a project that would remedy this situation. He organized a team of 'action' men which included the base doctor (for his invaluable knowledge of this subject), Ed, our Warrant Officer Radioman, and one of his crew, plus myself. We all agreed to keep this escapade a secret, at least until it was finished.

The start occurred when Dave 'acquired' a 50 pound sack of sugar, and a 25 pound box of prunes. I was delegated to buy some dates in Tunis and bought a 10 pound box, to add 'flavor'. I was also to beg, borrow or steal two really large earthen jugs with a capacity of at least 15 gallons each. This I was able to accomplish by a one month rental from a shop in Tunis. Ed was given the task of 'borrowing' a large pressure cooker from the galley. In addition, he went to the aircraft 'grave-yard' and acquired some good copper tubing to capture the vapors rising from the hot liquid in the cooker, being condensed as it traveled through the tube to a collecting vessel. This he added to the pressure cooker lid to complete assembly of a 'still'.

The earthen jugs were located in the basement of the building we lived in. Now the 50 pounds of sugar were divided between the two jugs, and similarly, the prunes and dates were divided and added. Now water was added to the 'mash' and left to start the fermentation process. (This had to have been done during warm weather, probably August or September '43, otherwise fermentation would not have happened).

Doc kept tabs on the fermentation process, and after about 3 weeks he proclaimed that the mash was ready for the next step. As I recall there were about 15 gallons of liquid strained out of those jugs, and these were brought to the waiting still. It was not possible to do the entire 15 gallons at once so several 'cookings' were done. A thermometer had been worked into the lid in order to control the temperature of the liquid being 'cooked'. The reason for this was told us by Doc, who said temperatures above 160° F would boil off fusel oil, which was a poison.

After cooking all the liquid, Doc tested the distillate and said we have alcohol at 50 proof. That was on the weak side so this liquid was put through the still again. This time Doc measured the output at 100 proof. Why not see what we could reach? So the liquid went back for a third cooking. This time Doc measured 180 proof and said that's as far as you can go. When this last cooking was going on, our radioman helper had taken a teaspoon and held it under the outlet of the cooling tube, and drank it down. He immediately screamed "I'm on fire" and ran for the water faucet and gulped a couple of glasses.

We wound up with 2 gallons of 180 proof alcohol, and decided for bottling purposes 90 proof was sufficient, so diluted it with an equal amount of water, winding up with 4 gallons of clear prune alcohol. It couldn't be bottled as gin, the taste was wrong. Doc came up with a suggestion that was followed, and that was to 'burn' some sugar in a fry pan, add some water, and you have a yellow-brownish coloring agent. This was added to the alcohol and now it looked more like whiskey. About 15 empty liquor bottles were filled, with their original labels undisturbed. A bottle with a Bourbon label was presented to the Captain, in private. He allowed as how, if he had been aware of the project sooner, he would have had to stop it because Navy Regs would not permit it; however now that it was done he was not going to pursue it.

The rest of the bottles went into the Officer's Club bar. During a subsequent party, an officer who was just passing through was asked if he would like a drink. He said, "Have you any Scotch?" and the bar tender brought out a bottle labeled 'Johnny Walker Black Label' and poured him a shot glass full. The officer gulped it down and said, "That's the best damn Scotch I've had since leaving the States". The team, all present, smiled a bit, but did not point out that this was un-aged prune alcohol, instead taking a bit of pride in their accomplishment.

A Visit to a French Artist'sHome

The artist's home

There were some other adventures that are worthy of recording, for instance, a visit to a well-to-do French painter at his residence, pictured above

The Artist with his easel

A shot of the Artist with his works. He enjoyed being photographed.

Artist with portraits

A woven wall Hanging

More of Artist's work

This artist, can't remember his name, was obviously talented and had prospered quite well, as shown by his house and its furnishings.

On the following page there are miscellaneous photos that may be of some interest to the reader.

Favorite scene: a Supply ship

Officers 'Skinny dipping'

Base HQ flag

Officer tourists at Roman ruins

French Foreign Legion fort

Boy leading bull

Arab boys

Arabic Architecture

The Boys are begging for candy or gum.

Local showing off his donkey

Letters from North Africa
1944

V-Mail Form
January 2, 1944

Dear Mom,

Today I received your V-mails of Dec. 11 and 13. I'm glad you liked the Christmas cards—No, I'm afraid I haven't enough ability to make any as nice as that. And also the water-color I sent Violet—that was done by a refugee Frenchman—I thought it was very nice too.

The last two days we have had a bit of rain and wind here—last night was quite cold, but today it seemed to get a little better—hope it stays that way now. We were supposed to take a little trip out to some interesting ruins today, but it was a little too raw and damp, so we put it off until another day when the weather will be a bit better.

The officer's name who called you up in December was Weigand, and he wasn't so young either—he is probably about 40 or so, but a nice fellow anyway. There is another officer on his way home who might call you up if he gets to New York - his name is Baumann, and he is a swell fellow too.

Guess I told you had a letter from Aleck—and I had a letter from Loren too—he is in England now, and seems to like it a lot.

I have been so busy lately I haven't had much time to write you letters but in a day or two, I will see if I can't write you a nice long one. This typewriter seems to be acting up a bit—hope it lasts until I finish up on this. There isn't much room left anyway, so I better close with all my love to Violet, Dad, and my favorite mother--

Arne

V-Mail form
January 11, 1944
Dear Mom and Dad,

I realize I have been rather lax in writing you lately, but I know you will forgive me. There have been so many things to do, as I've said before. These V-mails do not have much room, but they are a letter and they can be written in a fairly short time—I figure they are better than nothing at all. In the last few days, I have received many Christmas cards—many from people I hardly know. One of these was from Ben Dyrland, *(cousin Alf's brother)* another was from Mr and Mrs Oscar Sanne *(from church)*. It was nice to know that these people thought enough of me to send me cards, but it did seem a little peculiar.

We have had quite a bit of rain lately, and we even had a little hail a few days ago—some of the hail stones were as big as marbles. It has been somewhat cool too, but not as cold as New York or Minnesota at the same time of the year. In fact, a few days ago, I thought for sure that spring was here. The sun was shining all day, and it got nice and warm, but it didn't last, so we will have to wait a bit more I suppose.

I have been able to get quite a few more pictures, and when I next get a chance to write you a long letter, I will include some for your enjoyment. I'm glad Violet liked her water-color present, it wasn't much but it was something anyway. The money I sent you for a Christmas present wasn't what I wanted to give you, but there again I was stuck. I had Virginia buy a present for Aleck, and from a letter he sent me just a few days ago, he liked it very much. It was a wallet—probably something like the one she sent me for an Xmas gift.

There isn't much news from here—one of the officers in our division was transferred, and we miss him a lot. He was the one we called Smitty, that is another reason we have been busy lately, for he did a large share of all our work. Our wardroom (Officer's Mess) has had the addition of some new china, silverware, napkins, and tablecloths—so now we really have it pretty nice here. Last Sunday, we had turkey again, today we had roast beef, tomorrow we have roast pork—and I can't understand why I don't get fat as a little pig. But I have never felt better in my life, so you don't have to worry on that score. Tonight we had ice cream for dessert again—the first time in two months. Our mixer

117

went on the fritz some time back and it was only a few days ago that it was fixed again, but from now on we will have that for dessert twice a week.

Here we are again, down at the bottom of the sheet, so I will close with all my love to Violet, and best mother and dad in the world.

Arne

Here are some pictures I may have included in the next letter.

Large German cemetery

Officers' graves

Officers' graves

Enlisted mens graves

119

Another cemetery view

A LaGoulette scene

Outskirts of Tunis and Mosque

Dome of Mosque showing here

Tunis City scene

The palace of the Bey of Tunis*

*At that time the Bey was the ruler of the Arab (Kasbah) section of Tunis, and allowed officers to tour his palace. It was very ornate, but the most striking part was his bathroom, where the commode seat had a stuffed satin cover (to be gentle on his 'tushy'). The palace is now a museum and the Bey is gone. Marie and I visited the museum while on a cruise, which visited La Goulette and Tunis 65 years, to the day, after I arrived in Tunis on May 28, 1943.

V-mail form
January 15, 1944
Dear Mom,

Here we are again with a short little letter to let you know I am still in the best of health—and wishing I was with you. I haven't had much mail lately, but there must be a good reason for it—perhaps because I have not been able to write many letters myself!

Yesterday I took one of my usual business trips to the nearby base, and I received a very pleasant surprise. I met one of the fellows I went to school with out at Minnesota. We were in the same class in Naval ROTC. Of course, we had to have a long talk, and I invited him to come down and visit us. It was really swell to meet someone I knew from school.

I am having a cruise box built (more or less of a trunk). It will be made out of some very nice wood, and should hold quite a bit of my gear. I really need it too, because I have acquired such a lot of stuff since I left the States that the bags I have would never be able to carry it all.

The weather here has been just about the same for the last few days—sort of overcast and cloudy, with an occasional sprinkle of rain—and there *(will)* probably be lots more before we see real good weather again. But the days are getting longer, and that I like.

Just got my laundry back tonight—cost $2.50 but there was quite a bit of stuff there so it was fairly reasonable. Looking over my records, I find that my total earnings for '43 (not counting the uniform allowance) was almost $2100—pretty good for me, don't you think?

Not much room left on this sheet—must close for now.
Love to you all,
Arne

North Africa
January 23, 1944

The day after the start of the Anzio invasion - the reason for heavy work load.

Dear Mother and Dad and Violet—

Here it is the end of another day, and time to write to my favorite family again. The time seems to be going by so very fast—and you don't hear me complaining about that—the sooner or quicker the time goes by, the sooner I will be home.

As usual there isn't much in the way of news. Everything is going on much the same as always. Today we had turkey again for dinner—can you beat that? And our supply officer says there may be enough left over to give us another turkey dinner before it is all gone! Last night we had a really fine dinner too. There was roast pork loin, dressing, apple sauce, mashed potatoes, green peas, wonderful gravy, bread and butter, coffee, and for dessert, vanilla ice cream with a chocolate sauce—mmmm! I will be spoiled when I leave the Navy, we have everything so good.

We have a new chaplain on the base. The other fellow was transferred—and we hated to see him go for he was such a swell fellow. The new chaplain seems to be a very nice man too - he gave a very fine sermon this morning. He is a Presbyterian and come from the South somewhere. I still like Mike Silseth best of all the chaplains I have met.

I am sending you an enlargement I made a few days ago. It was taken on top of another mountain—we seem to be making lots of mountain climbing trips. Smitty took the picture with my camera, and then when it was developed, I did a job on it with the enlarger. Boy oh boy, I am going to have a great deal of pictures to show you when I get home again.

We are very busy these days, perhaps that's why the time seems to be going by so fast. I don't think I will have so many chances to go sightseeing anymore. But that remains to be seen.

Since you told me that George Lund went to Africa I have been meaning to take a trip not so far from us to visit an Army Air Center. A group just came from the States not so long ago, and I thought he might be with them. He probably isn't but there may be a chance that he is.

Today I got the last bit of lumber I needed to build my trunk or sea locker as we call them. It is very nice mahogany wood and should make a neat job. With that done I should have enough room to transport all my gear without any trouble at all. The carpenters here built one each for Mr. Long and Dave, and they did a very nice job on them—I think perhaps I will have the best one for I have the nicest wood.

All the boys have got to bed already, and I think it is about time for me to do the same—so good night, and pleasant dreams and –

Lots of love,
Arne

V-Mail form
January 28, 1944
Dear Mother,

Nothing much to talk about tonight, but thought I'd drop a few lines to let you know everything is fine. Your birthday card and Dad's and Violet's letter came a couple of days ago—and they were so very nice, all of them. Hope you didn't go to any trouble with the package—it hasn't arrived yet, but will probably show up in a day or two.

We have really been eating well lately. We have been able to get some fresh vegetables and eggs from the local markets to supplement our regular menu, and a few days ago we received a new shipment of fresh meats, eggs, fruits and other good things. And my appetite hasn't decreased at all.

As usual, I have been keeping busy, although I have found time to go out for a little target practice with pistol, and I have tried my hand at doing a little sketching again. My latest drawing isn't done yet, but it looks like it may be pretty good. A few days ago, I took a trip inland with some of the other officers to a French monastery—that's where I bought the eggs and really beautiful cauliflower. The trip was very pleasant, weather good, and we saw some interesting things. On the way we saw a camel caravan of about 20 camels. They were the funniest looking things you ever did see.

I suppose Aleck will soon be through with his new course. I haven't heard from him lately—how is he? Tomorrow morning I must make another trip so I must get some sleep.

Good night and pleasant dreams to all. Love to Violet, Dad, and of course, yourself.
                    Arne

V-Mail format
February 2, 1944
Dear Mom,

Another uneventful day has passed. Received your letter of January 12 yesterday, and I have a little scolding to do. Mother, I know you like to see my bank account grow, and I do too, but I insist that you take out your fifty dollars every month, because if you don't do it at the time, I just have to do it myself when I get back. According to my books, I should have 750 dollars minus what bills you have paid for me—and that should be well over 100. In other words, I should only have about 700 dollars in the bank, and by this time I should have repaid you a full 700 dollars too. Have you been getting my bonds regularly also?

Today, the captain had two WAC officers as guests for lunch. They were quite thrilled with the meal they had, and thought the Navy was pretty good. Our boys are having a dance on Valentine's Day and the WACs have been invited. Their officers said that the girls in the outfit would like to come to a Navy dance. And you can bet that our boys will make them feel at home.

Glad you like the pictures I send home. I would like to send more, but it is hard to get enough supplies to go around. Will send more whenever I get the chance.

My new sea chest is almost made, and it is going to be very nice. It is made out of mahogany, and is quite roomy. All I need for it is handles and a hasp, and I think I will be able to get them pretty soon.

Hope everything is going along well, and that everybody is feeling as well as I am. Love and kisses to Violet and Dad, and yourself.

Arne

North Africa
Feb 12, 1944

Dear Mom & Dad-

Seems like I'm always behind with my letters—hope you don't worry too much when there is a period of time between letters. We have been very busy again this past week—almost like last July—and that was a tough month. *(That was the Sicily invasion referred to, and this one is the Anzio invasion.)*

You see, our traffic went up—and since we lost one man about a month ago, the increased work had to be spread on the four of us remaining. But it has slowed down now, and we are beginning to breathe easier again. *(The traffic referred to included radio messages from small invasion ships that had problems that needed shore attention, all part of the Anzio operation).*

We have had very freakish weather during the past week— much rain and wind, sleet, hail, & even a little snow (which melted as soon as it hit the ground). It has been much colder than I've seen it before in Africa—but never went below freezing. You can bet we were glad to have the stoves. I can hardly understand how the natives and French around here can exist without any means of heating their homes. None that I have been in have had stoves or heating plants—a couple of them had small fireplaces, but they weren't sufficient to heat the room or house. I feel sorry for them sometimes.

Mike Silseth came down to visit me yesterday. It would have to be our busy spell—and I wasn't able to spend much time with him, but we did have a nice gab-fest for awhile. He & his friend hadn't had anything to eat all day (they came about 2 P.M.) so I went to the galley & rustled up some ham & eggs for them— which they enjoyed very much. He may get a chance to get back to the states in a month or so—hope he gets it. (And I hope to get a chance too-----)

You asked me if there is anything you could send me—I have everything I need except—one (1) set of pajamas. And if you could find me some flints and fluid for my lighter I would appreciate it very much. You won't have to send me anymore film, Mom; I have enough now – with what you have on the way in my birthday package and what I have on hand.

I am rather tired, so I will bid you all a pleasant Good-night. Love to you all, Arne

No.

To MRS. KARL G. JENSEN

825 - 7Ø STREET

BROOKLYN, NEW YORK

(CENSOR'S STAMP)

From

ENS. A. JENSEN, USNR
(Sender's name)

NAVY 94, C/Ø FLEET P.O.
(Sender's address)

NEW YORK, NEW YORK

FEBRUARY 18, 1944
(Date)

DEAR MOTHER,

RECEIVED YOUR LETTER OF FEBRUARY 3RD YESTERDAY, AND VERY HAPPY I WAS TO GET IT. MAIL HAS BEEN COMING IN PRETTY GOOD LATELY--AT LEAST IS SEEMS SO. MOST OF THE LETTERS SEEM TO TAKE ABOUT 2 WEEKS TO GET HERE, ALTHOUGH SOMETIMES IT TAKES LESS, AND SOMETIMES MORE.

I THINK MRS. ANDERSON MUST BE UP TO HER OLD TRICKS AGAIN, FOR I DIDN'T WRITE HER TWO LETTERS FOR CHRISTMAS--I WROTE HER A V-MAIL XMAS CARD AND THAT WAS ALL. AND HER BOY ROY IS ALSO IN AFRICA--THAT IS A SURPRISE. I THOUGHT THEY WEREN'T SENDING ANYONE ACROSS WHO WAS LESS THAN 2Ø.

THE WEATHER HASN'T BEEN SO GOOD THIS LAST WEEK--A MIXTURE OF RAIN, HAIL, SLEET, AND WIND--AND THEN SOMETIMES IT HAS BEEN LIKE SUMMER. I DON'T CARE FOR IT. THE CHANGEABLENESS IS VERY DISCONCERTING, AND MAKES PERFECT WEATHER FOR CATCHING COLD. SO FAR, I HAVE BEEN LUCKY ENOUGH NOT TO CATCH ANYTHING--HERES HOPING.

LATELY, I HAVE BEEN GETTING LESSONS IN FRENCH. ONE OF THE FELLOWS HAS A FRENCH GIRL FRIEND WHO SPEAKS FAIRLY GOOD ENGLISH, AND SHE HAS VOLUNTEERED TO HELP ME OUT. I HAVE BEEN ABLE TO LEARN A FEW WORDS, AND HOPE TO BE ABLE TO LEARN MORE. SHE IS A VERY NICE GIRL, WELL EDUCATED, AND VERY INTERESTING.

I HAVE THE TAX STATEMENTS YOU SENT ME, BUT I AM NOT GOING TO DO ANY-THING ABOUT THEM UNTIL I GET BACK--AND THEN I DON'T THINK I HAVE TO PAY ANYTHING. I SUPPOSE DAD HAD TO PAY QUITE A BIT OF TAX THIS YEAR.

WELL, THIS EVENING WE ARE HAVING A QUIZ PROGRAM BEFORE THE MOVIE, AND IT IS ALMOST TIME NOW. LOVE TO DAD AND VIOLET AND YOURSELF.

V---MAIL

The story below describes the lessons referred to in the above V-mail

The French Lessons

Some time in '43, we had made the friendship of some French girls. Lt . Kahn had invited 3 lovely young ladies to visit our base. He was dating one of them named Luisa. He introduced them all and Luisa soon approached me and in the resultant conversation she, of course, asked if I could speak French. When I told her, 'only a few words', she immediately offered to be my teacher of the French language. I told her that I would like to learn to speak French. And so arrangements were made to have me get those lessons at her home. This was in an apartment house in the Kasbah. Normal entry to the Kasbah was through the main gate, but she said there was a side door near the apartment that I should use, and told me how to find it.

On my first visit I met her mother (father was dead). It seemed as if she approved of me. Mother served us tea and some sort of cookie and then left us to the French lessons, in the living room, both of us side by side on the sofa. I had a pad of paper and pencil to write words.

We started with simple stuff, much like I was exposed to in learning English as an immigrant in 1927. I wrote down the French words, with her giving me the French spelling. During the lesson she would put her arm around my shoulders and cuddle up-- presumably to be sure I was writing correctly. That first lesson lasted about an hour, and arrangements were made for the next lesson the following week.

I went back the next week and was warmly greeted by both mother and daughter. The same routine was followed this time, and now I was also learning polite phrases, like 'pass me the butter please'. I can still say this phrase in French but can no longer spell it. Another hour of these phrases and it was time to go.

The next lesson came a week later and we were to continue with additional conversational phrases. We had been exchanging English and French words for perhaps 15 minutes when she excused herself and was gone for a few minutes. I thought it was 'a call of nature', and no problem. When she returned she excitedly said "Maman n'est pas ici" (Mama is not here, she is gone). And with that, quickly sat down next to me, put her arm around me and started kissing me. It took me a couple of seconds to realize the implication of her statement and her follow up actions. I had never before been so openly seduced. Many fellows would say, "Do it", but I immediately thought of Virginia, and even though we were not wed, I felt a need to be true to her. It was difficult to turn her down without hurting her feelings but somehow I managed to extricate myself. That ended the lesson for that day and basically for all time. It became evident that Luisa and other young women her age were angling for an American officer husband, and the bait was sex. Other officers reported similar experiences, and some took the bait but not the wedding vows.

However, the friendship relationship was maintained, and as you will have noticed in some of the previous and later letter transcriptions, reference was made to visits to 'our French friends'.

North Africa
March 4, 1944

Dear Mom & Dad & Violet—

I suppose I'm way overdue on a letter to you and if you are a bit peeved, I don't blame you. We have had another bit of tough luck – Lt. Long our boss was transferred last week, and also our yeoman (typist and file clerk) – and that made a lot of extra work for the rest of us. I do most of the typing now, and there is quite a bit to do.

Golly, it was just a year ago yesterday that I left home – and it has seemed like a very long time. And just a year ago tomorrow that we left New York. How well I remember getting my last look at the sky-line of N.Y. and Brooklyn. And it was an exciting trip. I remember how thrilled I was when Africa first came into view. And then the first month or so on land, everything was so strange and different. Well, I've gotten quite used to it now, and it almost seems like a normal way of life.

Did I tell you that last week my friend *(British)* Major DeBirney had me in town for lunch. He is a swell fellow, and sure served a nice meal. I received your birthday package day before yesterday—thanks a million. The talcum powder bottle had broken on the way, and there was perfume in the air as soon as they handed me the package. I now have enough film to last me for a while—please don't send anymore. And I am well stocked on everything else; in fact, I may send some of my things home because I'm getting too much to carry around.

My eyes are very heavy—must go to bed. Good night & love to all!

Arne

P.S (To Violet) Ma petit Violet, cheri. Je t'embrasse bien affectuesement!

The above post script was my attempt to demonstrate that I had learned some French.

North Africa
March 18, 1944
Dear Mother, Dad & Violet,

You will see from my return address that I am now at a new base. *(This happens to be Bizerte)* It is not very far from our previous location but this base is much bigger. I left Monday morning & arrived here in time for lunch—one of the best meals ever.

The day after, my room-mate, Dave Teske, came up and now we have a room together here. It is a large, airy, light room, with a small washroom for our private use adjoining it, almost like a kitchenette. And then there is a little ante-room where we hang our clothes and stow our suitcases & other gear. When I first moved in, there wasn't anything in the way of furniture there, not even any light bulbs, so I wrote a note to Dave and told him to bring all the furniture he could lay his hands on when he came up. And he did! He brought our beds, a wardrobe cabinet, 2 deck chairs & one other one, and a table & some bulbs. The next day we spent almost all day cleaning and fixing the room, and you should see it now, it's really very comfortable!

The officers' mess is amazing—almost like the best hotel restaurants in the States. There, in a large hall, with full length windows covering almost 2 complete sides, you have numerous tables, each seating 8 men. Fresh white linen tablecloths adorn each table, and a complete dish & silver service at each place.

The food is served by Italian prisoners of war, and they are excellent waiters. The food is marvelous!! Every noon we have soup, and the rest of the food is extra delicious too! If I don't gain any weight here, it won't be the fault of my appetite or the food.

The Italian prisoners come around to our room every day to clean it up & make the beds. It's just like living in the best hotels—only you don't have to worry about paying for it. Of course, we pay our mess bills once a month ($30) but that's all, and there is very little else to spend money for. Even our laundry is done free here!

Well, I must close for now, but will write again soon. Love and kisses to you all.
Your loving son & brother,
Arne

Dear Mom and Dad & Violet—

   Late again, but this time I have a pretty good excuse. I've been in the hospital *(in Bizerte base)* a week today. Now don't be worried—by the time you read this, I'll be out again and back at work. You see, almost 2 months ago something happened to cause this. I was lifting a crate, and just after it was in position on my shoulder, I felt something give down around my lower intestines. Next day, I went to see Dr. Montag just to be sure, and he told me I had a hernia—rupture you'd call it—and said it should be fixed. Well, I knew I was going to move soon, so we decided it could wait until I came up here. A week ago yesterday, I entered this hospital, and a week ago today Dr. McIntyre operated. It wasn't bad at all—there was some pain that day, but I've been feeling fine ever since. Today, the Doctor is going to take out the stitches, and in 6 more days he says I can leave. I'm glad it happened now & here—for now it has been done free of charge—and I've been getting the best of medical care you could ask for—the Doctor did an excellent job on me. I needed a little vacation anyway—now I've had time to do some reading and perhaps catch up on my writing.

   Everyone has been swell to me, practically all the fellows have been in to see me—Mr. Long, the Skipper, the Exec, Dave & Ed, Charlie, Mac, & a bunch of others. *(It was great to have them, and they took great delight in telling me jokes and funny happenings--to make me laugh, because when I did, there was pain in the wound. When I was finally allowed to sit up, I barely reached vertical and then fell back again. On the third try I was able to stay up and, with help, was able to get out of bed. The long stretch of 2+ weeks flat on my back was tough on the balance. This experience is in sharp contrast to a similar ruptured hernia repair in 1992, as an "Outpatient" operation. I was only at the hospital 5 hours and then I was allowed to be taken home.)*

   The mail has been very good this last week, and that made me feel very good. I've had 5 V-mails from you, one from Aleck, & a few other regular letters. By the way, what is Aleck's new address? I also received a box of cookies from Virginia, meant for my Birthday, but getting them now was just as good. And they were good too—not one of them broken, because she had wrapped each one separately with wax paper.

It must have been nice to have Aleck back again for a while—was it only a week he was home? I'm quite sure I won't be back for another 6 months—unless something unexpected comes up, but it is not worthwhile counting on that. Yup, it's been over a year now that I've been overseas. It hasn't been bad at all, and I'm glad I had the chance to do something like this. Because of this duty, I'll have certain benefits and privileges after the war that will be valuable.

Ed had some of the boys bring a radio over to me, and although it doesn't work so good, it provides some measure of entertainment. Yes, I really feel in good shape now, and there is no reason to worry in the least. Well, this must be all—will try to write again soon. In the meantime, keep smiling—and God bless you all.

Love,
Arne

P.S. Don't forget, the new address is: Navy 93, Box 5A
Fleet Post Office
New York

North Africa
April 5, 1944
Dear Mom & Dad & Violet,

Well, I am now out of the hospital & feeling fit as a fiddle. Of course, the Doc says I must take it easy for another 2 or 3 weeks—no work, no exercise, just loafing around. It will be a kind of vacation, and a welcome one at that. The only trouble is the "nothing to do". Well, the 2 weeks in the hospital went pretty fast, so I guess the next 2 will be just about the same. It's good to be up and around again—to get out in the sun and fresh air again!

For the time being, I'm living in a Quonset hut because I'm not allowed to climb stairs, and the room Dave picked out for us is on the 3rd floor. There are 6 fellows living here regularly, Ed being one of them. Yesterday, 4 ensigns who just came over moved in, and you can tell they are new in the Navy—just like a bunch of high school boys. The other men are a pretty nice bunch though, and get along well together.

I have a pleasant surprise for you—won't tell you quite yet, but as soon as we find out for sure I'll let you know. I'm afraid it isn't that I'm coming home, although I sure would like to tell you that.

The weather is getting to be very pleasant—the sun shines warmer, and more often, and the rains are not so frequent. In another month we will have to start going around in shirt-sleeves, maybe even sooner than that. And the fields and hills are a riot of color—all sorts of flowers are coming up, and it is really gorgeous to see that after these months of drabness.

I received quite a bit of mail while at the hospital, and that made me feel very good, of course. And did I tell you Virginia's box of birthday cookies arrived while I was there?

Everybody in the hut is out tonight except myself. They all went over to see the movie, but I wanted to catch up on my letter writing, so I stayed here. It seems like I'll never be able to catch up on my correspondence, but an attempt must be made. It was pretty hard to write while in bed, and now is a good time to do it.

News is so scarce, nothing much happens to break the routine. Must try to write a few more letters now.

Love to you all, Arne

Print the complete address in plain block letters in the panel below, and your return address in the space
provided. Use typewriter, dark ink, or pencil. Write plainly. Very small writing is not suitable.

No._____

(CENSOR'S STAMP)

To MRS. KARL G. JENSEN
825 - 70 STREET
BROOKLYN, N.Y.

From
ENS. A. JENSEN
(Sender's name)
NAVY 93, BOX 5A
(Sender's address)
FLEET P.O., NEW YORK, N.Y.

APRIL 9, 1944
(Date)

Dear Mom,

Just a little note to wish you a happy Easter. Our Easter has been very quiet — It rained most of the day, so it's a good thing no one was wearing any of the usual new clothes. This evening tho, it is pretty nice out — the sun is shining again, and a nice fresh breeze blowing.

You should have seen all the sailors at church this morning — it would have done your heart good. Every seat was taken, and the fellows were standing all around — in the door and a large number outside the door. It was a communion service, and everyone partook — I imagine there were better than 300 men there, and that was only one of the services. So you see, the boys keep pretty close touch with the church, even tho they are far away from home.

There hasn't been any mail this past week, but it probably will turn up soon. I am feeling very well now, this little rest is doing me a lot of good. Regards to all and God Bless You!

Love,
Arne

V-MAIL

North Africa
April 12, 1944
Dear Mom & Dad & Violet—

How is my favorite family these days? Feeling as good as I am, I hope. I've had 2 letters from you, Mom, in the last 2 days. The mail is finally coming addressed to this base. Yesterday the airmail of April 2 came—that was only 9 days, and that is plenty fast. Say, incidentally, you don't have to use the 8¢ airmail stamp when you write to me or anyone in the service – the 6¢ stamp will do—just ask the postmaster, he'll tell you.

I understand your writing perfectly Mom – don't ever worry about that—sometimes I wonder if you can read my chicken scratches. Say, that bank account of mine really sounds OK— golly, I never thought I'd save so much in so short a time. It's perfectly all right about the way you handled the insurance, but it seems to me you should have kept the money because you paid the premiums. But don't forget, on my next check you start taking out the $50 a month again—I insist on that. Pretty soon I will buy some more bonds—my pay is accumulating here, because there is nothing to spend it on, and it will help the government out that much more. If people would only understand that to buy less now—to squeeze & deprive themselves, they would be so much better off later on, for it would help prevent a dangerous inflation, and give them more to buy the nice things that will be made after the war.

Will you see if you can get me Roy & Anna's address—I'd like to write them—and Aleck's new address too! Yes, my sea chest is finished, and it is pretty nice – I can pack lots of things in that. Soon as I can, I'm going to start sending some of my stuff home so there won't be so much to lug around—there's lots that I never use.

I'm glad to hear Violet is wanting to go to college – more power to her—fine idea. If she does, I will help as much as I can. How about sending her to Minnesota? It's a wonderful place – and Virginia would look out for her. Be good for her too!

I'm feeling great now – the doctor said I was about the best patient he ever had. Will start work next week, and that will be fine with me—I've rested long enough.

Must go to bed now—Sweet Dreams to all of you!
Love & Kisses, Arne

No. _____

[CENSOR'S STAMP]

To MRS. KARL G. JENSEN
825 - 70 STREET
BROOKLYN, N.Y.

From
ENS. A. JENSEN
(Sender's name)

NAVY 93, BOX 5-A
(Sender's address)

FLEET P.O., NEW YORK

APRIL 15, 1944
(Date)

Dear Mom,

Another beautiful day drawing to a close -- looks like Spring is here to stay for awhile. No mail today but perhaps tomorrow there will be some.

Today I did a little laundry -- some underwear, sox, and hankies. The laundry does a good job, but the white clothes come back with that "tattletale" gray look, so I'd rather do that stuff myself. And today I used the sewing kit you sent me -- I was trying to repair the button holes in my blouse. It wasn't such a fancy piece of work, but it will make the holes last a bit longer anyway.

Tomorrow I go back to work again, and don't you think I'm mad about that? It's been all of a month now since I was on duty, and believe me, it will feel good to get back on the job. I'm going to see the Doctor again for another check, and then it will be just another memory. Hope everybody at home is in good health. Don't let Dad overwork himself -- he should get more sleep. And take care of yourself too -- and Violet!

Love to you all,
Arne

140

No. | To MRS. KARL G JENSEN
825 - 70 STREET
BROOKLYN, N.Y.

[CENSOR'S STAMP]

From LT.(JG) A. JENSEN
(Sender's name)
NAVY 93, BOX 5A
(Sender's address)
FLEET P.O. NEW YORK,
APRIL 27 1944
(Date)

Dear Mom,

Work is again taking up quite a bit of my time, but I am enjoying it, for it is much better than loafing and doing nothing. Had some letters from you, and Violet and Dad recently -- many thanks. And the package with the pajamas, flints and cigarettes came about a week ago. Thanks a million. But please don't send cigarettes any more for we can buy all we want, and at a much lower price than you have to pay.

I saw Red Mackay tonight -- same fellow I saw once at the first base I was at. You remember him don't you? He was the tall red-headed fellow Aleck and George Lund sometimes went with -- they played soccer. He hears from Jimmy Hansen quite often, and we exchanged news from home. He is the first and only fellow I've seen over here who I knew back in the States.

I will have Saturday and Sunday off, so I am going to do a little traveling and visiting. It will be nice to get away for a bit. Hope everyone at home is well.

All my love,
Arne

V---MAIL

141

North Africa
May 5, 1944

Dear Mom, Dad & Violet –

It's a beautiful day out – sun shining, nice and warm, and a clear sky. Yesterday, after lunch, I took one of our deck chairs out on the roof—took my shirt off and sat there reading a book. It was so nice to feel the warm sun on my body again. It won't be long before I'll have another dark tan like last summer. This week I work from 4 till midnight—which isn't so bad, for you have daylight to do some of the things you like to do. One of the fellows wanted me to go swimming with him, but thought I'd better ask the Doctor first to see if it is all right. I guess there will be lots of chances to go from now on.

I had a letter from Aleck just a few days ago which he wrote from Kansas. He certainly has seen a great deal of the states, Texas, Oklahoma, Kansas, Tennessee, Georgia, Louisiana, and all the others he has passed thru. That's one thing I'd like to do when the war is over – do some traveling to the various states.

Last weekend I had two days off, so I rode down to our old base with the messenger. It was swell to get back there—it was such a nice place, and we had such good times. I also visited some of the French people I knew—the girl who was teaching me French, and some others that had been to the base. They were glad to see me, and told me to come and visit them anytime I was there. The ride both ways was also thrilling. You should see all the wildflowers growing around the countryside. There were acres and acres of them—all kinds: poppies, daisies, pansies, sunflowers, and many more. The roadside was just a solid mass of color—reds, yellows, blues, etc.

Around here, life goes on as usual—work, eat, sleep. We have had some busy days lately, but we are on definite shifts, and when our 8 hours are up, someone else takes over. I like the work, but I'd still much rather be doing some sort of engineering work.

Must go now—the Italian prisoner has just come in to clean our room, and I've got to get out of his way.

My love to you all,
Arne

North Africa
May 18, 1944

Dear Mom –

Guess I better explain the presence of the money order first. What with increase in pay and money that has been accumulating, it got so that I had more than $100 in my wallet—and since I didn't need it, thought it would be safer to send it home. You can put it into my bank account, or if you can use it, you keep it and we will consider it part of my repayment to you. In either case, let me know what you do with it – and if you don't mind, tell me every month when you make the allotment deposit how my bank account stands. It makes me feel good to know that I have a "nest egg" stored away—something I can fall back on when I return. And I hope your bank account is growing too – it is such a comfortable feeling!

I guess it won't be until late Autumn that I will have a chance to come home. That may seem like a long time now, but it will pass before you know it – and then more than likely they will give me a 30 day leave, and probably next duty in the States. Wouldn't that be swell?

Yesterday I had a day off—what do you suppose I did? Well, my laundry has been accumulating, so I washed out some sox and underwear. Then I took a cot out on the roof in the afternoon and lay there in my trunks for a couple of hours soaking up the sunshine. I am starting to get a nice tan already, and in no time, I'll be as brown as an Indian. My face has a very good color already, and if it gets much darker, you won't know me back. You know, God has been very good to me – I'm in perfect health now, eat well, sleep well, enjoy my work, and I'm as happy as is possible under the circumstances. Sometimes I wonder if I deserve having it so good. And I hope you people back home have it just as good as I do.

Well Mother dear, I have a few more letters to write. I'm getting behind again. My thoughts are with you all.

Love,
Arne

North Africa
May 25, 1944

Dear Mom –

Another week has gone by—time seems to go very fast, and that doesn't make me mad!

We are having such wonderful weather now—perfect spring weather. It makes a person feel glad to be alive—to be able to enjoy all the wonders of God's earth. And this strange country has a particular fascination all its own at this time of the year. It is so different from any place I've yet seen!

This last week I've been on the mid-watch -- from midnight until 8 in the morning. It is the first time in 2 years that I've had to be on duty all night. At our last base, we had night duty, but generally we were able to arrange it so that we could get 5 or more hours sleep every night anyway. Here, that is impossible – for a number of men must be on all night. It isn't so bad tho, once you get used to it, and you can get enough sleep during the day to meet your needs.

Mom, I wonder if you would try to get me a pair of nail-clippers or two. I lost the set I had, and it is quite a job keeping my nails neat without them. And if you would try to get me a leather wrist watch band. I could use that too – the one on my watch now isn't much good anymore. It should be 5/8 of an inch wide at the place where it is fastened to the watch. These are the only things I'd like to have which I can't get over here. Thanks much.

Tomorrow I have a day off, and will take another little trip. It should be lots of fun – hope the weather keeps on being nice. Must go to bed now.

Love & kisses to you all,
Arne

Dear Mom & Dad & Violet,

Today was kinda tough – worked from 8 this morning until just a few minutes ago, and it is now 10:15 P.M. I did get out for a few hours – on business – but it was a pleasure to get out of the office – got a chance to drive Mr. Long's jeep.

This job of mine isn't too difficult, but so many little details to worry about, and so many responsibilities. Now for another week or so it will be pretty easy, and then in another week, I'll have to work long hours again. Oh well, it could be worse.

Well, the big invasion *(June 6, 1944 on Normandy beaches)* has begun in France – and I guess your prayers are with our forces as well as mine and millions of others. Maybe it won't be so long now, but it probably will be longer than we expect.

Received your letter Dad, about 3 days ago—and a V-mail today from you, Mom. The V-mail was dated 2 June, and that isn't bad – just one week. Hope the mail service continues to be as good as it has been.

Do you know, I weighed myself recently – and now I weigh 160 lbs., about 12 more than when I left N.Y. And I feel good physically too! I am not as happy as I'd like to be, but then that is to be expected. When I get home, it will be different! You should see the nice tan I have now. My face is real brown and my hair has bleached some, and the French girls think it is a very nice combination. Bet you wouldn't recognize me if you saw me.

Tomorrow I am getting the day off and am taking another little trip to visit some of my French friends. Must go to bed now and get some sleep.
Love to you all,
Arne

North Africa
June 17, 1944

Dear Mom, Dad & Violet –

We are having such lovely weather nowadays. It isn't too warm yet, and in the evenings it is delightfully cool, wonderful sleeping weather.

We have been pretty busy again, but I like my work pretty well, and the time flies by. Today is the 15th month anniversary of my arrival in Africa. Guess I'm getting used to it now, for I hardly think of it any more. From what I've heard tho, I don't expect to get back for another 6 months or more. Golly – sure wish this war was over. There I go – I shouldn't even be thinking about it, for that makes me a little blue.

Had a very enjoyable weekend. Went down to our old base for a visit, went swimming for the first time this year, and was it nice. And my tan gets darker every day – you should see me now! Then we looked up some of my French friends and took them out to dinner at the Officers Club. They have such wonderful meals there. It hardly seems like we are in the war here.

Look Mom, you mentioned something about not taking any more out of my checks. I want you to stop thinking such nonsense. According to my books, you have only received $950, and it is probably only $850 because there were a couple of times you didn't take anything out. And I owed you $2000 from school, so you will keep on taking out $50 every month for at least one more year. If you don't need the money, put it in your bank account or buy bonds with it. Then after the war, you can buy yourself a house, or anything else you might want. You must promise me you will continue to take your $50 out every month – that's the way I want it to be.

Sorry to hear *(cousin)* Bendik was burned – hope he is better now.

Have to get a little sleep now. Pleasant Dreams to you all.
Love
Arne

146

North Africa
26 June 1944

Dear Mom & Dad & Violet –

How are things in Brooklyn? Here, the weather gets warmer every day, and the work goes on with monotonous regularity.

Received your letter with the application for a War Ballot. I'm sending it in – because I definitely want to vote this year. It sure would be swell if Aleck came thru here, but I guess there is little chance of it – for this place is well behind the lines of fighting & the air commands are generally closer.

Believe it or not, we had a little bit of rain in the last week – very unusual for this part of the world – it's been over a month since we last had any. It was nice & refreshing, but I contracted a bit of a cold from it. In my present healthy state, it will be gone in no time.

Yes, I've been taking my sun bathing gradually & now I have a beautiful tan. You should see my face – it's getting just about as dark as that of the Arabs, and my hair has bleached a little.

Last Friday night we had a dance at BOQ, and Dick & I took some of our French friends there. I wore my white uniform for the first time & was told that I looked "quite snappy" in it. It was nice to dress up for a change, and it is a very nice uniform. Wish we had more opportunities to wear them. But they get dirty so quick here – mine is in the laundry right now, and I had to spend a half hour cleaning up the white shoes.

This afternoon Dave & I were out on the roof soaking up some sun & with a shower after, it certainly felt fine. Think it will help my cold too.

In an earlier letter, you told me about my bank account Mom, and it really makes me feel good to know that I have a good savings account. Too bad I'm not married – I'd be getting $96 a month more. I know it costs money to support a wife, but in a situation like this, the wife would probably be working, and that would also help. No sense dreaming about that tho – I'm not married, and that's that.

Kinda tired tonight, guess I'll get to bed early and get a good night's sleep.

Pleasant Dreams to you all from - your loving son &
brother, Arne

North Africa
July 6, 1944

Dear Mom & Dad & Violet,

We have been so very busy lately – the only way I can get to write you a letter is to take a few minutes off from work and type out a few lines. Received your letter of June 29 yesterday, and that is very good time – hope our mail always gets here that fast...but it probably won't.

It has been terrifically hot here for the last week or so. We don't use any covers at night any more, and then we are still warm. In the day time it is fairly nice in the morning up till about nine o'clock, but after that, the air is like a breath out of a furnace. Our uniform regulations have been relaxed somewhat, so that we can be a little more comfortable. We don't have to wear our blouses any more – except when we have liberty off the base. And we don't have to wear ties except at meal times. We are even allowed to wear shorts, if they are regulation.

Our food has improved lately, and has become just the right thing for this type of weather. For lunch we have a green salad, a sandwich, a light dessert, and iced tea or lemonade. At supper we have the heavy meal, with soup, meat, potatoes, vegetables, and the rest.

I'm glad to hear that Jackie *(cousin Jackie Johnsen)* is getting his wings—don't know why, but I wasn't sure he'd make it. Guess he feels good about that, and bet Tante Malena and Uncle Jack and Vivian are plenty proud of him.

This week it has been hard for me to get time to write to anybody for Dave has the mid-watch and likes to go to bed after supper, and since I work in the day time the evenings are my only free time. It is such a funny arrangement, but then we have to make the best of it.

I haven't felt so good this last week either – have had a light summer cold, and a slight touch of dysentery. However, I am just about rid of both of these ailments now, and am feeling pretty good again.

Thanks for your V-mail letter Violet – wish I could answer every single letter I get, but that would be very difficult, and I guess I will just have to combine my letters to you and Mom, and Dad.

Last night we had the most beautiful moonlight night you ever did see. The moon was full, and it was just about as bright as the day time. And when the moon beams shone on the water, it was just as if there were a million stars dancing around on the ripples and waves.

It is almost time for lunch – will close for now.

Love to you all,

Arne

North Africa
July 14, 1944

Dear Mom & Dad & Violet –

I can hardly believe that one of my letters reached you in three days but I'm very glad that it did—and I hope all my mail to you goes that fast. And you Dad, said one of them came in 4 days – well, as long as they get through in that short a time, we can't complain a bit. Most of our mail comes this way in 6 or 7 days – sometimes up to 10 days but mostly in a week, and that we like too.

I'm very happy to hear that Jackie J got his wings – that's pretty good all around for our family, isn't it? I suppose he will have 3 months or so in the States for further training before he is shipped out.

I've been meaning to write Aleck for some time now – but we have been so very busy. Today I had half a day off – and what do you suppose I did. Well, in the afternoon, I visited my room-mate Dave, who is in the sick bay (they thought he had the beginnings of pneumonia, but it was just a case of exhaustion, so he will be OK after a few days rest). Then I came back to the room and took a nap until supper.

After supper, we played some ping-pong, and then I came up to the room, and did laundry for an hour and a half. Washed 5 sets of underwear, 2 cap covers, 2 handkerchiefs, and some socks. And this afternoon I brought a big bundle of my khaki uniforms down to our regular laundry. After washing this evening I had to take a shower because I had perspired so much during the day. And now I am just about ready for bed.

Mom, I wonder if you would get me some air mail stationary with the Navy insignia if possible, a bottle of Schaeffer's V-mail black ink, and some more flints for my lighter. And if you go over to New York, stop in Macy's uniform shop (or any uniform shop) and see if you can get me one regulation white shirt to go with white shorts. It is more or less of a sport shirt – short sleeves, open neck. You know my size I guess – 14 neck. Thanks in advance and don't forget to take the bill out of my allotment or bank account. (Don't buy the shorts, because I bought a pair here.)

And now to bed.

Love,
Arne

151

DEAR MOM, DAD, AND VIOLET---

TODAY I GOT A NEW TYPEWRITER FOR MY WORK, AND I THOUGHT
I WOULD DROP YOU A FEW LINES JUST TO TRY IT OUT. I MAY MAKE
A FEW MISTAKES BECAUSE I AM NOT QUITE USED TO IT YET--BUT IN
A SHORT TIME I SHOULD BE DOING ALL RIGHT AGAIN.

WE HAD A TURKEY DINNER AGAIN YESTERDAY--ALMOST EVERY
SUNDAY WE HAVE TURKEY--AND THE BEST ICE-CREAM I HAVE TASTED
IN A LONG TIME. YUP, WE ARE EATING VERY WELL--FRESH VEGETABLES
AND GREEN SALADS AT ALMOST EVERY MEAL.

MY ROOM-MATE DAVE HAS BEEN IN THE SICK-BAY FOR THE LAST
FEW DAYS. THE DOCTORS THOUGHT HE HAD THE BEGINNINGS OF
PNEUMONIA AT FIRST, BUT IT TURNED OUT TO BE NOTHING MORE THAN
A CASE OF EXHAUSTION--THE GUY HAD BEEN GETTING ALONG ON ABOUT
4-5 HOURS SLEEP OUT OF 24 FOR THE PAST MONTH OR SO--CLAIMED
HE COULDN'T SLEEP ANYMORE THAN THAT. BOY, I NEVER HAVE ANY
TROUBLE SLEEPING--I AM ALWAYS WISHING FOR MORE TIME TO SLEEP
IN.

IT IS GETTING WARMER AND WARMER EVERY DAY. HOPE IT
REACHES A PEAK AND THEN STARTS GOING THE OTHER WAY SOON.
ONE DAY THIS WEEK WE ARE GOING TO HAVE A LITTLE BEACH PARTY
AND PICNIC AFTER WORK. WE ARE GOING TO GET SOME FOOD FROM
THE GALLEY, BRING OUR SWIMMING SUITS, AND STAY UNTIL ABOUT
EIGHT IN THE EVENING.

THE NOON WHISTLE IS JUST ABOUT TO BLOW, AND THAT MEANS
LUNCH--AND I AM HUNGRY! WILL WRITE SOME MORE SOON.

LOVE TO YOU ALL,

Arne

North Africa
July 27, 1944
Dear Mom, Dad, and Violet—

I'm sorry I haven't been able to write sooner and more often—seems like we have to work more and more as the time rolls by. Last night I worked until 10:30, and some of the other nights this week it has been almost as late.

Got your package yesterday – with the book, watch-strap and nail clippers. Very nice! I like the watch strap very much – just the right color and size. The book I haven't been able to look at yet, don't know when I will get a chance to read it.

It still is very warm here, and it doesn't look like it will cool off for some time to come. Dave has been going swimming right outside our door, but I don't care to do that because the water isn't as clean as it should be. Instead, I lay out on the roof, and soak up a little sun, if I finish early enough in the afternoon.

Tonight I have been invited to have supper with an English Naval officer – and see their movie afterward. I think I will go, for it is one of the few chances I have for relaxation – and I'll get a chance to learn more about the British. This fellow is a pretty nice fellow – he comes over to my office once a week on business – that's how I got to know him.

(At this dinner it was customary to propose toasts while drinking wine, like, 'Long live the King', or 'Here's to 'President Roosevelt' After several of these, my friend who served in Egypt, proposed this one:

Here's to the love life of a camel,
which is more difficult than one thinks,
for in a moment of amorous passion
the camel made love to the Sphinx.
Now the Sphinx's posterior channel
was clogged by the sands of the Nile,
which accounts for the hump on the camel
and the Sphinx's inscrutable smile.

This was so good I had to remember it by writing it down.
Obviously this was not included in the letter.)

There is such little news for me to write about – everything goes about the same – work, eat and sleep, or have I told you about that already? In the morning I get up at 7:00 and take a shower, eat breakfast, work until noon, eat lunch, rest a little from 5:00 until supper (at 6:00), then either work some more, or write a letter, and then to bed. Not a very exciting life, is it?

I had another letter from my friend in Australia – he says he has been there for 28 months now, and still no outlook of getting home. Of course, he is in the Army, and a non-combatant, but still it doesn't seem fair that a fellow should have to stay over that long. I don't think I will have to stay that long, in fact I am sure of it, but I still don't know when I will get my chance either. Hope it won't be too long. I could use a little vacation right now!

Still have a few things to finish up before I quit this afternoon, so I better say "good afternoon" and close.
Love to you all,
   Arne

Dear Aleck –

Have been meaning to write you for quite awhile – but only during the past week has work slowed up enough so that there is time for correspondence. I've even been neglecting Mom & Dad, and that isn't good.

It may be that I'll get home this fall – prospects look pretty good, but it probably won't be before October. And that will make 20 months or more overseas for me. Then I should be due for about 30 days leave – two weeks of which I'd probably spend home and the other two weeks in Minneapolis. Virginia said she would save her 2 weeks vacation until I came back, and oh boy, if that works out I could sure have a good time.

The mail just came – and I had a letter from Virginia saying that she had had lunch with you. I'm certainly glad you got up there and had a chance to meet her. And now that you have met her, Aleck, what do you think of her? An honest, frank, and unbiased opinion is desired. Also had a letter from Mother saying that she is fixing up the house in anticipation of your return late t his month. I'm going to send this letter to Brooklyn on the chance that you will beat it quicker that way.

Your trip to Cuba must have been interesting – and I can sympathize with you on the 17 hours without any sleep. I won't have half as much to tell about as you will when this is all over. It's been quite a while now since I've been off the base, and there is so little we can do for entertainment & relaxation. Don't have any facilities here for indulging in my photographic hobby, and even if there were – we've been working so much that we only want to rest in our spare time.

Last time I was out was almost 2 months ago when Dick Baylis & I took a couple of French girls to a dance here. We dressed up in whites – had a darn good time, but they lived 60 miles away & the traveling back & forth took some of the fun away.

Now that the operation has started against Southern France, the prospects of my getting back in late fall are even better, but I'm not placing too much hope in it for I've been disappointed too

many times before.

It's about time to quit for the day – give my love to the folks, and – have a good time on your leave. Be sure to send me your forwarding address so I can keep in touch with you.

Arne

Original V-Mail, scanned

TO
MRS. KARL G. JENSEN
825 70 STREET
BROOKLYN, 28
NEW YORK, N.Y.

SEE INSTRUCTION NO. 2

FROM
LT (JG) A. JENSEN, USI
NAVY 93, BOX 5A
C/O FLEET POST OFFICE
NEW YORK, NEW YORK
(Sender's complete address above)

AUGUST 20, 1944

DEAR MOM,

IT IS REALLY HOT HERE TODAY--AND IT HAS BEEN THE SAME FOR QUITE SOME TIME NOW. DOESN'T SEEM LIKE THERE WILL BE ANY LET UP FOR A WHILE EITHER--DAY AFTER THE DAY IT IS THE SAME. I'VE HEARD FROM OTHERS THAT IT HAS BEEN THE SAME AROUND THE EAST COAST TOO LATELY. IN YOUR LAST LETTER YOU TELL ABOUT SITTING AROUND OUT IN THE BACK YARD TRYING TO KEEP COOL--COULDN'T YOU AND VIOLET AND DAD TAKE OFF A WEEK AND GO UP TO NEW CITY, OR SOME OTHER PLACE LIKE THAT? IT WOULD DO YOU GOOD.

I SUPPOSE ALECK IS HOME NOW--SURE WISH I COULD BE THERE TOO, AND MAKE IT A REAL FAMILY REUNION. PERHAPS IT WON'T BE SO VERY LONG NOW BEFORE I GET A CHANCE TO COME HOME. THERE IS NOTHING DEFINITE ON THAT SUBJECT, BUT FROM ALL INDICATIONS, WE THINK IT WILL BE BY THE END OF THE YEAR--PROBABLY BEFORE CHRISTMAS--WE ARE HOPING ANYWAY!

DAY BEFORE YESTERDAY I HAD MY FIRST DAY OFF IN ABOUT TWO MONTHS. ANOTHER FELLOW AND MYSELF MANAGED TO GET A CAR, SO WE TOOK A LITTLE TRIP DOWN TO THE BIG TOWN TO VISIT WITH OUR FRIENDS THERE. WE LOOKED UP MISA, AND SHE GOT US AN INVITATION TO GO OUT FOR DINNER. IT WAS TOO GOOD TO MISS, SO AWAY WE WENT. IT WAS A GOOD DINNER TOO--ROAST RABBIT--SOMETHING I'VE NEVER HAD BEFORE, AND IT WAS GOOD!! WE ALSO HAD SOUP, TOMATO AND GREENS SALAD, AND THEN THERE WAS SOME KIND OF BAKED FISH PATTY. FOR DESSERT THERE WAS AN UNUSUAL KIND OF PASTRY. TASTED ALMOST LIKE A DOUGHNUT, BUT IT LOOKED MORE LIKE A SMALL ROLL. AND OF COURSE, WE FINISHED UP WITH GRAPES AND COFFEE. IT WAS NICE TO GET OUT--AWAY FROM THE BASE--TO DRESS UP (I WORE MY WHITES AGAIN) AND VISIT WITH FRIENDS . WISH I COULD DO IT MORE OFTEN.

OTHER THAN EVENTS LIKE THAT, LIFE STILL GOES ON IN THE SAME OLD MONOTONOUS FASHION--NOTHING NEW OR EXCITING. HAVEN'T BEEN ABLE TO GET OUT SWIMMING EXCEPT FOR ONCE THIS YEAR--EVEN THOUGH I HAVE BEEN LAYING OUT ON THE ROOF GETTING A BIT OF A TAN. MAYBE ONCE A WEEK I WILL GO TO A MOVIE, AND SOMETIMES ON SUNDAY EVENINGS THERE IS A RE-CORDED CONCERT OF GOOD MUSIC.

THE NEWS GETS BETTER EVERY DAY--PERHAPS IT WON'T BE LONG BEFORE THE GERMANS GIVE UP, AND THEN THE JAPS WON'T HAVE LONG TO GO EITHER. I HAVEN'T SEEN BERNIE YET--THOUGHT HE MIGHT BE OVER HERE AND TRY TO LOOK ME UP.

WELL, TIME TO FINISH UP--LOVE TO YOU ALL AT HOME.

HAVE YOU FILLED IN COMPLETE ADDRESS AT TOP?

V - MAIL

HAVE YOU FILLED IN COMPLETE ADDRESS AT TOP?

Dear Dad –

Guess it's quite a while since I wrote you a letter, although everyone at home is included when I write to Mom. However, this one is special for you – to wish you a very Happy Birthday. I only have one opportunity each year to send you such good wishes, but that doesn't mean that I don't think about you at other times, and wish you well.

It is probably more than a week now since I wrote home and I hope no one has been worrying. You see, the morning of Aug 25th, I received orders to make a little trip – to take officer messenger mail to one of our other bases, and to have a little vacation too. So I have been away from here for 5 days. The Captain has been pretty nice about giving us a little rest & change. Well, as it was, I flew up to Corsica – stayed overnight with some of my friends there, and the next day flew up to Naples, Italy. It was the first time I had been out of Africa since I arrived and it surely was interesting! I tried to get up to visit Rome, but that wasn't possible – however, I did see Rome from the air on the way because we flew almost directly over it. Naples is a big city and in some sections very modern & up-to-date.   It reminded me in many ways of New York. While there, I did quite a bit of shopping – there are many nice things to be had, quite reasonable too! It was almost like a Christmas shopping tour for me because that's what the articles will be, I guess. I had a good time bargaining with the shop keepers, and surprisingly, most of them spoke English. The town was kinda dusty & dirty, but there were lots of people around – some well dressed, others in rags, and it was very interesting to walk around and observe the people, the way they walk, talk & act, and to find out what they think.

My room-mate, Dave, and a couple other fellows I know were also up there on a trip, and when they decided to visit Pompei, I went along. We saw Mt. Vesuvius, which had an eruption last February (you probably read about it – spread dust and ashes almost 3 ft thick for miles around), and after a half-hour ride came to Pompei. We had an Italian guide take us around and tell us about the place. The ruins there were in a better state of preservation than any I've seen over here, and so much more interesting when you have someone tell you the history of the

158

place at the same time. It took about 2 hours to go around it, and even then we didn't see but a small portion of it all.

What gave me the biggest thrill was the 1000 mile round trip by airplane. It was so interesting to see the various lands & ocean underneath – to see the mountains and valleys, the fields & rivers, the roads & cars on them that looked like tiny ants moving along – and the cities and towns and villages looking like little models I've seen in some museums. It showed me how tiny and insignificant we humans are, and also how much we've accomplished. It was almost too much to take in at once, but I'm glad I didn't miss it, for it was by far the best experience I've yet had over here.

And the news these days is even better than remarkable. Today we had a report that the Yanks in North France are only 25 miles from the German border. There is good reason to believe that they can't last much longer – and that the war in Europe will soon be over. I still can't say how it will affect me, but it is just about certain that I'll get back before Christmas this year – and is that going to be wonderful!!! In a few days it will be 18 months since I left the States & that's quite a long time.

Well, it's about time to close for now – give my love to Mother & Violet – and I hope that your birthday is a pleasant & happy one, and that you'll have many, many more of them!

Your loving son,

Arne

Some additional info about this trip will add some further insights. It was a small courier plane that flew me to Corsica. And I was allowed in the cockpit. As we approached the landing strip on that island, I was able to see that it ended at the base of a steep mountain side. And while the pilot tried to set down as close to the shore (beginning) as he could, we continued rolling until we stopped just a few yards from the mountain—what a scare! The next morning at take- off time, the plane had been manuevered back to the upper end of the runway as close to the mountain side as possible, and the plane was heading down to the seashore end. The wheels lifted off the ground just feet from the water! A real adventure!

The visit to Naples was fascinating, One of the things I didn't describe was a visit to a restaurant with a buddy officer. There we had real Italian spaghetti with their meat balls, and a bottle of Chianti wine, the kind that comes in a bulbous bottle with the bulbous part surrounded by a woven fiber net. Both were delicious. One other thing I would not write home about was in walking in the downtown area, we were accosted many times by young (8 -12 year old) boys who would say, "Hey Joe, (all Americans were Joe) how would you like to buy my sister—she is very pretty, only $5", and there were some who said 'mother' instead of sister. It was obvious that they would do most anything for money, and not surprising because the war had created many desperately poor people, and there was not much paying work.

The Pompeii visit was much as described in the letter; however, I left out descriptions of some of the erotic wall paintings we saw, and the baths and other sexual symbols. Again there were young boys with the same mechandise as in Naples, and also selling 'fertility symbols' (a gold colored erect penis with scrotum and wings at the base), hanging from a chain. The young hawkers would call out, "Hey Joe, wanna buy a flying cock-and-balls?" This was supposed to be a help for young married women who wanted children.

Marie visited Pompeii while on a 2008 cruise (I could not goon the tour because of having to use my walker, and the tour director advised against my going). These are pictures she took.

Pompeii street scene.

160

Street carving pointing to brothel (to guide foreigners)

North Africa
Sept 9, 1944

Dear Mom & Dad & Violet –

It sounds like thunder outside, and it's warm & sticky in here, perhaps we'll have a little rainstorm. Hope we do for that would cool us off a bit. It has been so very warm for the last month or so - in fact, all summer.

Well, I now have 18 months of overseas service in, and theoretically am eligible for return to the States. However, we have heard nothing on the subject, and probably won't for a while yet. Virginia wrote & asked what I'd like for Christmas, and I think I ought to tell you the same as I told her – and that is not to send anything. There are good possibilities that I will be home by then, and if not, it wouldn't be long after that – in which case, they could wait until my return.

Wish I could have been home while Aleck was there. Bet you were glad to see him. It is so long since I've seen him now that I can't remember how long it is – 3, 4 years probably.

A few nights ago, we obtained a pass to go into the Kasbah (Arab-town) to see the festival which they are now celebrating. It is called the "feast of Ramadan" and lasts for about a month. It is a harvest festival, and during this time the Arabs do not eat or drink between sunrise & sunset. It was an interesting visit – the streets were all lit up and decorated, and there were people out everywhere. We went into one place where there was an orchestra & a dancer. It was funny to hear the weird oriental music all in a wailing, sing-song minor key – and to see the dancer go thru these peculiar steps. She sang songs as she danced & the audience joined in with her. I've learned a lot about these people – their customs and traditions, and I'll be able to tell you a lot more when I come back.

I think I told you that we have been going to the beach quite often, and that I have acquired a good tan. The exercise & fresh air, of course, are just as good for us as the fun we have. And it's one way of cooling off too.

About time for bed now.

Love to you all –

Arne

North Africa
September 16, 1944

Dear Mom and Dad and Violet –

Today we had some mail, first for about a week now, and it was nice to hear from the home folks again. I received your package a few days ago, and all came thru fine—the ink bottle didn't break as you thought it might. I took your box of cookies down to my French friends with me last Saturday, and they were really thrilled about them – also some chocolate I had. You know they can't get chocolate at all, except as gifts from us, and it is a very great delicacy for them. I still have the one box of cookies left for myself tho, and I am saving that for the time being.

The figures that Violet sent on my financial accounts are interesting—if true. I'd like to have her work for me as my book keeper some time—I'd sure make a lot of money pretty easy. There is one thing that bothers me a little. On Sept. 3rd, 1943, I sent home a check for $77.50, and on her list it was missing. What I am wondering is whether you ever received it or not. As I remember, you did say you received it for I can't find the receipt for it and I usually save all receipts until I hear that you have received them. As a matter of fact, I don't quite understand about that insurance money. I thought that you were giving me a hundred dollars of that and Violet has listed it as going to you. And if that is wrong and you put the 100 dollars of the insurance money in my bank account, then she shouldn't have subtracted the amount of my bank account from the total received, because it isn't listed under receipts which it should be in that case. And there is also a certain amount of interest which must have accumulated on that bank account which should not have been included when the subtraction from the total was made. (Only the deposits should have been subtracted from the total received.) I know we will get the whole thing straight when I get back, but from my records here is the way it should stand (approximately).

- 7 one hundred dollar checks sent home $700.00
- 1 check for $77.50   77.50
- 13 allotment checks   1300.00
- 1 check from U. of Minn.   13.22
- 1 deposit of $100 for insurance (to me)?   100.00

163

Total money originally belonging to me	$2290.82
Expenditures (as listed by Violet)	142.61
Net amount originally belonging to me	2148.21

Outside of, or not counting the $100 insurance share, there were 20 $100 checks sent home, of which you should have taken half, Mother, or a total of $1000 each, for you and me. However, there were 2 or 3 times as I recall that you put in the whole hundred dollars in my account, and there were a few times that you just paid the insurance out of the 100 dollars and put the rest in my account. You can better tell me those cases, because I didn't keep track of them. And I almost forgot the fact that the $100 for uniform is also included in the bank account. If we subtract that amount and the insurance check, that leaves about $1250 that you deposited out of the money orders I sent or the allotment checks, right? (The $36.53 left over is probably part interest, and part incidental that I can't figure.) And that means that you have kept $750 for yourself instead of the $584.08 that Violet figured. Maybe I am mixed up, but I guess we will find out sooner or later. (Don't tell Violet, but I think she was trying to gyp me – only teasing).

Nothing much new to tell—it gets dark quite early now, and we have stopped going to the beach. Sometimes we play horseshoes after work, but it gets dark so quick, that we hardly can see where we are throwing the shoes.

My room-mate Dave managed to get some Coca-Cola for us last week and that really tasted good for a change.

I have been quite busy lately again – had to come back here and do a little extra work tonight, and probably will have to some more of the same to keep caught up on my work. Oh well, I've done it before, guess I can do it again.

It is getting late now, and I had better get some sleep so that I will be fresh for tomorrow's work.
Good night and love to you all!

Arne

North Africa
Sept 26, 1944

Dear Mom –

Another week gone – one more week closer to home. No indication yet of when it will be, so we'll just have to keep on hoping. A few days ago I packed up my books & some Electrical Engineering magazines, and some of my extra clothes and sent them home addressed to you. When I do travel, I want to have as little to carry around as possible. Probably very soon I will send some more. You must not assume from this that I know when I am coming, or that it will be very soon, because that is not so – I just want to be prepared whenever the occasion arises.

The weather has at last become delightfully cool, such a pleasant relief from the summer heat. There have been some rather strong winds, and we've had a bit of rain too, but all in all, it is very nice here now.

Our friend Smitty has rejoined us after an absence of over 6 months. He was with us at "94" *(La Goulette)* you know, but left in January to go in a ship and take part in the invasions. Now he has been reassigned to our base, and we are glad to have him back. He told us some hair-raising stories of those invasions & I am very glad that I didn't have to take part directly. The last one *(Salerno)* was quite easy, he said, but the other one at Anzio was plenty tough. He spent most of his time running to and from the air-raid shelters.

This coming Saturday, 2 of my friends & I are going to try to make a trip. It is such a long time since we have gone anywhere around this area, and there are a couple of spots I have wanted to see for a long time. We will have a picnic lunch fixed up & stay all day. Hope the weather continues to be good.

There is a souvenir shop which has recently been opened on the base, & they have some marvelous things bought in Egypt, Malta, Italy, India and other places – and for very reasonable prices too. I hope to get some, but there are so many others here who have the same idea, and there may not be enough to go around.

Well, it's about time to take a shower, and then get to bed. Good-night and love to you all.

Arne

North Africa
Oct. 9, 1944

Dear Mom & Dad & Violet –

Here I am – late again. I hope you haven't been worrying, and I know it was thoughtless not to write, but there has been so much to do. The end of the month was the end of the third quarter, and that meant more inventories, reports, & other special little things to do. It was only today that I finally finished up on that, and tomorrow I can go back to the old routine again. Actually, I am supposed to have an assistant – a yeoman. However, there hasn't been one available, so all that extra work I had to do anyway. Oh, it isn't so bad—sometimes the job can be swell, other times I'd just as soon be doing something else.

We have been having good weather the past week or two – a few days of rain, but on the whole it has been perfect. It has been cool enough so that we don't melt away, and grand sleeping weather, but not so cool that we can't go around in our shirt sleeves. In the evenings, if we have occasion to be out, we have to put on jackets for there is a chill in the air. There will probably be lots more rain pretty soon tho.

Last night I washed some of my clothes out—and was wishing I had Mrs. Kossart's *(U of M rooming house owner)* washing machine handy. You remember my speaking of her – she was my landlady out at school the first 2 years. Golly, that brought back some very pleasant memories too.

You know Mom and Dad, I've been thinking. And the more I think the better the idea seems to be. When this is over, and prices have gone down again, Aleck & I will buy you a farm somewhere – there are some very good spots in Minnesota, and other places. It is possible to get one fairly reasonably – and just think, you could raise vegetables & chickens – maybe have a cow. You'd have enough food to keep yourself and more left over to sell. And I sort of think it's the kind of life you would like to live – clean, fresh air and all that. Of course, there are many angles to it, and it requires more thinking and investigation, but you'd be free, independent. Tell me what you think of the idea.

Saturday, I am going to have my first day off for some time now. I am planning on going down to the big town *(Tunis of course)* with Smitty and visit some of our North African friends.

It's always nice to get away from the base for a day & we are looking forward to it.

Nothing more on our going home, but I'm not putting any faith in getting back by Christmas. Only thing we can do is hope & pray. God bless you all.

All my love to my favorite family -

Arne

October 21, 1944

Dear Mom & Dad & Violet –

It is finally turning quite cool – in the morning & evening anyway. During the day it is still warm enough for shirtsleeves (when it isn't raining) but that probably won't last so long. How is everything out your way? Hope the hurricane didn't come up to New York this time!

Yesterday, I sent another box of things home to you – my white uniform & shoes (which I won't use until next summer), my khaki & white shorts, 5 white shirts, the linen collars (I have enough paper collars to last me), a couple of towels and a pillow-slip. There are still some more things I want to get back, and will probably send another package shortly. Then when I do get a chance to go home, there won't be so much stuff to take with me. I am planning to leave the old suitcase (the big one we bought when I went away to school, made out of cardboard) here because I have the sea-chest that was built for me, and the old thing isn't worth taking back.

I also cut down my allotment from $100 to $75. I did that because lately I have bought so many presents that Dave had to loan me some money to tide me over. And then too, the amount I am getting now would certainly not be enough when I get back. However, I still want you to continue taking $50 out of each check for yourself, and use the $25 for paying my insurance or putting in my bank account. Please now Mom, do it that way and not the other way around.

Please Mother, and Dad & Violet too – don't count on my being home for Christmas. There is a small chance that I will get back by then, but very very small indeed. However, I do think that my birthday will see me back home. Oh, it would be wonderful to be home for the Holidays but – then there still is work to finish here.

I've been quite happy lately – my work is all caught up and I have some help. (Although I could just about do without it now – sometimes it is a hard job to find something for him to do) and I don't have to work so hard myself. The only thing that hasn't been so good is the mail situation. Only about 5 letters in 2 weeks & I generally get twice that much. But then it's the same with the

168

other boys too, so we know it must be poor Uncle Sam's overloaded postal system, and not our correspondents.

Time for bed – Sweet Dreams to you all. Love,

Arne

Dear Mom & Dad & Violet –

We've been busy again, or I should say yet – seems as tho the work never stops coming in. Last night I worked just about till supper time, and then perhaps should have gone back after – but was so tired, I just went up to bed. Today, there was no let-up – I worked every minute until 4, then took the rest of the afternoon off to play some tennis with Mr. Long, Smitty & Dave. It's the first time I've had any real exercise in months, and I think it did me good although I know I'll be stiff as a board tomorrow. It's fun, and we are going to play some more.

Last week I received a box of cookies from Virginia – and were they good! They were Toll-House cookies, you know – the kind with chocolate chips in them & a few raisins. You know, Violet, if ever you want to win a boy's heart and affection, one of the things that helps a lot is to be a good cook & baker – the old saying that "The way to a man's heart is thru his stomach" is just as true as it ever was.

A few days ago, I did a really big washing – about 7 or 8 sets of underwear & about a dozen pair of sox – and if you don't think that kept me busy for a little while you're mistaken. But now that I am all caught up, the soiled clothes are starting to collect again, and if I don't hurry & do some more, there will be another big pile of it.

Did I tell you that we are all now restricted to the base? There is a rather bad epidemic running in the nearby towns, and although we've all been inoculated against it, they are not taking any chances. It's kind of tough in one way, because now we can't visit our friends any more, or take trips on an occasional day off. Guess it's the best thing tho, no sense taking any chances. So now when we have some spare time, there isn't much to do – perhaps a movie (which doesn't interest me much any more) or read a little, or sit around & talk awhile, or write letters – our recreation is fairly limited.

I'm thinking that perhaps I will be here to get your packages – at least it looks that way – so don't get your hopes up only to be disappointed. Seems rather sad to think of spending another Christmas away from home, but things could be much worse.

Chaplain Silseth has gone back to the States – I think he has been home 3 or 4 months now. Virginia sent me a clipping saying he was regional chaplain for 5 Midwestern states – that sounds pretty good.

It was sad to hear that Bob Deedee died – he was such a young boy. All I hope is that all this is not in vain, and that there won't be another world conflagration in another 20-30 years.

Oh yes, we have three chapels on the base – one Protestant, one Catholic, and one that is used jointly. They are all very nice, and full up every Sunday.

It's near my bed time, and I am very sleepy. God bless you all & keep you.

All my love,

Arne

North Africa
Nov 10, 1944

Dear Mom & Dad & Violet –

I am a little blue tonight – don't know why – perhaps it is a bit of homesickness – mixed in with some loneliness. And perhaps it is because I feel guilty in not writing you oftener too – here it is 10 days since the last letter I wrote. Perhaps you can sympathize with me tho – there is nothing to write about but the never-ending round of work, eat & sleep. Since we have been restricted to the base on account of the epidemic in the nearby town, we can't visit our French friends any more, and since there has been so much work, there has been no time off in the last 3 weeks or so. A rather sad situation.

A few days ago we received some more inoculations and vaccinations. If the holes in our arms didn't heal up quickly we would look like a kitchen strainer before long. But I guess it's better to be safe than sorry. We think the restriction on leaving the base will be lifted in a couple of weeks – then we will be able to get a little relaxation and visiting in again.

One of my friends from school showed up again a few days ago, and we had a good time last night when he came over to have dinner with me and talk awhile about old times.

The base is already planning a Christmas party for all the needy children in the area. We have been asked to donate old clothes, extra candy & things like that, and the Sea-Bees are going to make toys for them. Last Christmas there was such a party, and it was probably the best some of these kids ever knew. We are going to try to make this one the best of all.

The weather has turned cold and raw, with quite a bit of rain. We have steam heat in our rooms, but not quite the kind you have. These radiators only take the chill & dampness out of the air, and do not actually heat the rooms. But we have lots of good warm clothes so there is no need to worry about that.

Just before starting this letter, I had been cleaning up some work which I couldn't get at this afternoon – so today again, I worked 10 hours or more. For the past week or so I've had to be up at 6:30 and at work by 7:15 and will have to continue like that for some time yet. It is now after 10 PM, and time I went back to the room & to bed.

Sleep well folks, and God Bless you all.   Love, Arne

North Africa
November 16, 1944

Dear Mom & Dad & Violet –

Today has been a very nice day – not so cold as a few days ago, and with the sun shining brightly. In fact, there were a couple of fellows out on the roof this noon taking a sun-bath – can you imagine that!

I've been very busy at the office again – the work keeps rolling in with no end in sight. I was promised some help last week, but so far it hasn't materialized. The little yeoman striker they did give me to help out couldn't do any of the things there was to be done, so he was transferred to another department. It is kind of tough to know you are falling behind in work and not be able to do anything about it.

I received the package you sent from Abraham & Strauss a few days ago. It must have gotten wet coming over because there was a bit of mold on the cake, and it also must have been in a warm place because the candy had melted. It's a shame – I had to throw it out – all except the two jars of marmalade – it would have been very good, all of it.

A few days ago one of the fellows I went to school with passed thru here – on his way home. He had only been over here about a year, and now he is on his way back – some fellows get all the breaks. Of course, he is on one of the landing ships, and I don't envy him that job – so that evens things up.

I hope Aleck gets to stay in the States over Christmas and has a chance to go home. I'm afraid I won't have that chance, and will make you happier if one of us is there.

Last night some of the boys came up to our room and we had a little game of bridge – then we talked awhile – someone brought in cheese and crackers and we had a little coca cola for an evening snack. Then we harmonized a little on some old "barber-shop" quartette songs, and had a very enjoyable evening. It's really fun when a bunch of fellows you like get together and have a good time. There is so little we can do for recreation around here. I've done a little reading, but there isn't much time for that.

Time for bed – Good Night & sleep well!

Love,

Arne

174

North Africa
November 26, 1944

Dear Mom & Dad & Violet---

I have just about finished working for the day, and thought this would be as good a time as any to write you a little letter. Received a letter from each of you yesterday, and another one today. It was really sad to hear about Roy's death *(Roy Andersen, not Lindberg)*. I can remember him just as well as if it were only yesterday that I saw him last.

We had a very nice Thanksgiving here. Church in the morning was very crowded – there were two services held. We did not have the big meal at noon, but saved it for supper. Of course, we had turkey, but first there was soup, stuffed celery, lettuce salad, olives, then the turkey and spiced ham, baked potato, buttered peas, carrots, and pie and ice cream for dessert. And with the coffee, they passed out cigarettes for everybody. It was a very nice dinner as you can see, but I was wishing I was back home instead.

The weather continues to be very good for this time of the year. We haven't had much rain lately, and the sun has been shining, and it has been fairly warm. Somehow or other I have caught a little cold tho, and I have been rather miserable for the past few days. It is beginning to break up now and it will probably be gone before very long.

A few days ago, the ban on leaving the base was lifted, and now we can go to one of the nearby towns. Last night we drove up to the Allied Officers Club on the seashore just to get away for a lot of fun. Some of the boys drove out in the afternoon and went out to one of the beaches we used to go swimming at last summer. Of course they didn't go in – just went out for the ride, and they said it was quite rough there – waves 10 feet high.

I am glad to hear you finally got my second box. Perhaps I shouldn't say "finally" for it seemed to me it got there pretty quick for parcel post – just about 22 days. Tell me, was everything in those boxes that was listed on the sheet of paper I had left on the inside? Or did it look as if the boxes had been opened for inspection? I was just wondering about that – some of the fellows

175

who sent boxes home have received letters that there were things missing from them. Hope everything was there.

And Aleck hasn't left the States yet. Well, he is just as well off there – hope he stays for quite a while yet. I am going up now and catch a short nap before supper – maybe that will help shake that cold of mine.

Love to you all,
Arne

Dear Mom---

This letter is just for you – for your birthday. There are no birthday cards available here, but then there isn't a birthday card made that could say just the right things for you on your birthday. And this typewriter isn't much of a help either, what with the dirt it puts on the sheet (from the stencils I cut) and the limitation of expression.

But you know Mom, however poorly my words read, that I still love you and remember all the things you have done for me. I couldn't begin to list them all – there are so many that come back on the spur of the moment, and if I thought a little more I am sure there would be enough to fill a book. Most children take mothers for granted while they are at home, and it isn't until they are away for a while that they start to miss all the little things only a mother would do for her children. I guess that is true for me too, and although I can take care of myself quite well, I still miss having someone take care of my clothes for me, bring me afternoon coffee and sandwiches….and all the other things that go to make life at home mean all that it does. Of course, someday the children grow up and get married, and then someone else does all those little things – but it never is as good as "mother" does it. "Mother" is the best cook, baker, laundress, tailor, housekeeper, and best everything.

And Mother is the one who takes care of her little ones too. When they fall and scratch their knees, or bump their heads, or skin their noses, she is the one who bandages the injury. When they are sick, she is the one who sits by their bed and strokes their fevered brows with her cool hands. She's the one who tucks them in at night and says their prayers with them. She is the one who sits up and waits for them if they stay out too late, and keeps the supper warm if they have to work overtime. I could go on for a couple of hours this way, but still wouldn't be able to cover everything.

And needless to say, God was very kind to me when he gave me the best one for sure. I have often wondered whether I deserved such a blessing, and many times have thought not. But I certainly wouldn't trade you for any other

177

mother on earth. So here is wishing you a very Happy Birthday, and hoping that you will have many, many more of them!

Your loving son,

Arne

Dear Mom & Dad & Violet –

Today I just received your letter of Nov. 20 – the one in which you told of Roy Anderson's death and sent the Memorial service bulletin. It was very sad to hear of it, and I imagine it must have been pretty hard on the Andersons. It was a very fine letter Harold wrote to his folks and it must have meant very much to them. God grant the war will be over soon & bring an end to this senseless slaughter of the world's best.

I received the two food packages you sent about a week ago. Thanks a million. We will have lots to eat now, in fact with all the things you sent, a box of goodies from Virginia, and another package of food from another girl *(Jean Anne Rice)*, I sure have a lot. And the other fellows also received much food by mail. I am putting some of mine in the collecting can - presents to the needy French and Arab children – I could not possibly eat it all myself, and would feel very guilty if I did. So far, there has been quite a bit collected – food, clothing & candy, and some of the sailors are building toys for the tots. I think it will be a very nice Christmas.

I am losing my room-mate, Dave Teske, after being with him for 19 months. He is not at all well, and is being sent to a Naval hospital where they can make a thorough check. He will more than likely get home within a month – and I am glad for him because he is a swell fellow and will have a better chance of getting well there. His leaving means that I will have to wait a little longer, because although I was on the list to go home, we will be one man short now, and therefore my name was scratched off. But I don't mind so much – when I think how much worse things could be. And staying here a little longer may mean the difference between getting a 14 day leave or a 30 day leave, -- and also between being sent out to the Pacific or getting a shore job in the States. In one way, I was sorry to see Dave go because he and I got along so well, and we had such many good times together. I'll miss him and his good humor. My new room-mate is a nice fellow too, a psychologist and a very smart boy. I think we'll get along well.

I haven't been working such long hours lately – pretty well caught up at work now – but the boss still won't give us any days off. I've been catching up on my sleep, trying to catch up on laundry and letter-writing, but still have some to go.

I sent you a little package a while back – it may not reach you before Christmas but I sure hope so. The things weren't much – just a few of the souvenirs I picked up in Italy, but I hope you like them.

Time to wash out a few more socks before bed. Good Night…Mom, Dad & Violet, and a Blessed Christmas Season for you with the New Year bringing Peace.

Love & kisses,

Arne

NOEL 1944

Stars of Christmas burning bright,
Keep your Vigil through the Night.
Lift our hopes and blaze our way,
Take us to the Peace of Day.
Bring us home from lands afar.
Light our way, O Christmas Star.

Merry Christmas to Mom & Dad
Arne

No. _____

(CENSOR'S STAMP)

To
MISS VIOLET JENSEN

825 - 70 STREET

BROOKLYN 28, NEW YORK

From
LT (JG) A. JENSEN
(Sender's name)

NAVY 93, BOX 5A
(Sender's address)

C/O FPO, NEW YORK, NY

CHRISTMAS, 1944
(Date)

Christmas Greetings

V - MAIL

Love,
Arne

182

Dear Mom & Dad & Violet –

I'm coming home!! Within a few days I will be leaving, and expect to be home sometime in the last half of January. I'm so excited I can hardly eat or sleep. It has been a long time in coming but at last the end of my days in Africa is in sight. My packing is all done – spent about 4 or 5 hours on that job – washing some clothes too, so that I wouldn't have to pack any dirty ones. And today I sent another box home, containing 3 khaki trousers, 4 shirts, the old blanket you gave me, 1 book, and 3 Elect. Eng. Magazines. Perhaps that will arrive about the same time I do.

Believe it or not, today I got a letter from you dated August 2nd. You had sent it to Navy 39 instead of 93, and it had travelled around for 4 months – it had been practically everywhere. But it was still nice to get it. Told how hot it was, and how you and Violet were ironing in the basement, and Aleck freezing his feet from high flying.

I was supposed to have given a lecture on my job to a class of officers yesterday – but it was called off because of turning over the work, packing and all.

Don't write anymore, because it will just have to be sent back home. I'll try to drop you another letter before I get back, but if you don't hear from me, don't worry because I'll be on the way.

All my love – till I see you –

Arne

I did not know when I wrote the letter above that I would get orders late the next day, to board an LST for transport to the United States. What a thrill that was! As the above letter says, I was all packed and ready to go.

A request for a weapons carrier to transport me and my 'stuff' to the dock where 'my ship' was docked was granted, and there was a seaman to help get my baggage on board. When I stepped aboard, I turned around and a last look at my base at Bizerte was taken with some bemused thoughts; gladness, of course, but also a sense of loss, for I had made many good friends in Africa, both service people and French.

On board I met one other officer passenger, and seven enlisted men on their way home. Of course I met the captain, a newly minted Commander (three full gold stripes on his blue uniform sleeves). He was anxious to get under way and soon we were looking for the other ships of this convoy to be. It wasn't long before we were part of a convoy of five LSTs, several supply ships, and five destroyer escorts. The trip through the Mediterranean to the Straits of Gibraltar was quite smooth and pleasant. When we got into the Atlantic the wind became stronger, the sea rougher, and we were on the edge of a hurricane for 4 days. During that time the only hot food we had was coffee made in an urn locked in a cage. We subsisted on sandwiches. The ship was rolling almost 45 degrees either side of vertical, and it was very unnerving when there was a slight hesitation at the end of the roll, as if the ship was deciding to continue rolling or go the other way.

One other detriment to what should have been a happy journey was the captain, who was an avid bridge and card player. He insisted that the other officer passenger and myself take part with him and an off-duty crew officer in a game of bridge. He didn't buy my lack of experience in the game and said that stakes were only a tenth of a cent per point so that the cost of losing would be minimal. The second day we played the rolling got so rough that the cards were sliding off the table and he gave up that game. After three days of playing I was really anxious to get out of playing and told him so. He showed his anger but did not press the issue. We finally passed the storm and were now closing in on our destination, the Norfolk, VA, Navy base. Approaching it, an enlisted crewman turned on a radio and at that moment I heard the Andrews Sisters trio singing a song I will long remember,

"Drinking rum and Coca Cola". It was such a refreshing sound of home. After docking we could not go ashore until customs inspection was complete and here I was in a dither because I had a German officer's 9mm pistol, in a leather holster and 2 extra magazines. The customs inspection was quite casual, to my relief, and we were allowed to leave the ship on Dec 22nd. We were met by a seaman with a weapons carrier and he took us to the local BOQ (Bachelor Officers Quarters). Since there was no way I could make it home that day, I decided to stay overnight, and enjoy looking around town. We went downtown and went to a recommended restaurant where I had a jambalaya shrimp dinner which was such a delightful change from ship menus.

The next day we again had a seaman and weapons carrier take us to the railroad station. I bought a ticket for Pennsylvania station and had a porter help get my gear on the train. Can you imagine my feelings as that train approached home? I had called Mom and told her my approximate arrival time. When I reached Pennsylvania Station, I realized I could not go home by subway with a sea bag, large suitcase and large heavy sea chest, so I had a porter take my stuff to a taxi stand, loaded me up and the cab took off for Bay Ridge, Brooklyn.

Mother must have sat out on the steps of 829 70th street for some time, and when she saw the cab pull up she came to the curb, eyes streaming, and waited for me to come out. Upon exiting the cab I embraced her, and held her for a full minute, feeling her quiet sobs. What a glorious moment! Then I realized I had to pay off the cabbie. Pop and Violet came and the embraces were repeated. What a delightful homecoming! And for me and the family, **a fabulous Christmas gift.**

There were many poems I wrote at times when I was lonely and blue. Since these were times when I was thinking of Virginia it is not surprising that some will be identified as being written for her, and of course included in letters to her.

A Nightmare?
This was for Virginia

Last night, as very often of late,
I saw you in my dreams. It seemed
As though you beckoned me —
From a far off place — a city.
But what a city! A soul-wrenching sight—
With battered streets — and shattered parks,
And houses torn to bits — gaping windows
Staring sightlessly at the desolate scene
In mortal anguish.
The iron birds of prey had come and gone —
Had come to hover for awhile —
And lay their deadly eggs. A nightmare?
I saw you standing there—among the ruins.
My heart stood still as I approached;
Could it be? — Was it true? – But sighed,
"Thank God!" when you came near, unhurt.
Unhurt? No, not bodily, but worse.
Your eyes told me — pain, more horrible
In its muteness. For all things dear to you
Were gone — erased — home, family, friends —
All things worth living for. I groaned,
"Oh God, why must these things be?" —
Then trembled — and with a start, awoke! —
And drenched in sweat, I thanked my Lord
It had been just a dream.

Brooklyn, New York,
Feb 18, 1943
Written two weeks before sailing
to an unknown destination

186

Dissertation on Women

Women are such funny things,
They're very unpredictable —
For often you meet one who clings,
And sometimes one who's amicable.

And there's the type who's very bright,
And loves to keep you guessing —
And others that are not the type
A man would call a blessing.

They all use powder, rouge and paint
To keep themselves from fading —
And there are those who act the saint
When Boyfriend likes some necking.

Some are boring, dull and dumb,
And others very clever —
Some are tall, or short, or plump
But admit it, they will never.

They really are peculiar folk,
We'll never understand them —
But we'd not have it otherwise,
They're really swell—— God bless 'em.

(Written in answer to "Dissertation On Men" sent to me by
Virginia)

Arzew, Algeria
May 1943

Has It Happened To You?

Has it happened to you —
That a flirting smile,
A certain walk and air,
Of someone you know
Should upset you so —
Could it be that love is near?

Has it happened today —
That a thought persists,
Of someone who's far away,
Who was once so near
Does it now seem clear —
That he has not gone to stay?

Has it happened at last—
That Dan's arrow struck
Like lightning from above?
Not much you can do
If these things are true —
For it sounds to me like love.

Arzew, Algeria
May 1943

188

Dreams

This evening on the seashore of the blue and gentle sea,
A thought takes shape, a vision forms, of home — and you —and
me.
The vision clears — it seems so real—— it's hard to understand
That far away across the sea, there is my native land.

The days gone by pass in review — they seem like yesterday,
The things that meant the most to me — of work, and rest, and
play.
Of times when you and I went out – to dance or see a show.
Of times when we would walk and talk, when moonlight was
aglow.

It doesn't take a lot of thought to look along the past,
But more fun still it is to think of when I'm home at last.
To dream and plan of future days when this Old World is free,
And happiness will flood my heart—— if you will marry me.

Arzew, Algeria
May, 1943

The Many Little Things

The many, many little things,
Which don't amount to much.
A cheerful word, the song one sings,
A little gift and such.

A flower for the one who's sick,
A laughing, twinkling eye,
Just one of these will do the trick—
Dispel a care or sigh.

And if you add them—— what a sum
It finally will be.
Believe me, it will soon become
A wondrous sight to see.

La Goulette, Tunis
June 1943

190

A Wanderer's Promise

Another day, in months gone by,
We were together — you and I.
We walked and talked along a road,
Where clear and sparkling waters flowed.

The splendor of the rolling plain,
Some day we will enjoy again.
The countryside all dressed in green
Will greet us with the sun's bright sheen.

The flowers with their petals rare
Will nod their heads without a care.
The birds will sing among the trees.
What can be better than all of these?

When I return back home some day.
With thankful heart, I'll surely say,
"No other place I care to see.
I'm perfectly content to be, at home."

This is where I will always be.
I've traveled far and wide to see
The lands of ancient history.
No more will I this wide world roam.

La Goulette, Tunis
June 1943

Flanders Field in Africa — '43

The field lay quiet in the dark,
The birds no longer sang;
The moon came up, the graves to mark—
Where once Mark IVs did clang.

The '88s no longer roared,
Nor did the rifles crack;
The screaming shells no longer soared,
Nor was there any flak.

The dim of battle now was gone,
Yet on that quiet field
Our boys, who died there, still fought on —
To make our vict'ry sealed.

We must not fail them, we who live,
Or else they died in vain;
We must make sure our all we give
To free this world again.

The eulogies we sing for them
Will mocking, empty be —
Unless we win the peace for them
For all eternity.

La Goulette, Tunis
June 1943

The African Fly
(With apologies to Ogden Nash)

The fly is a pesky little insect,
Especially the African variety.
It is persistent as all heck-t
And doesn't know the meaning of propriety.

No matter how much you shoo them,
They return to sit on your physiognomy,
To calmly explore you, it doesn't phase-em,
And they just rub their legs in glee.

You can spray them and swat them,
Try anything else you can think of,
Though you take careful aim, the swatter will miss'm
And the spray, it seems, is what they like the stink of.

So the African fly, in my estimation,
Is a pest, and pain, if you please,
For even after much altercation,
It will not its annoyances cease.

La Goulette, Tunis
June 4, 1943

193

The Portrait

The portrait hanging on the wall
Brings mem'ries sweet and tender;
A touch of pain I too recall,
A tear unshed that will not fall,
Reminds me of the sender.

And oft I think of you at night,
And days of one December—
When we walked home one snowy night
In bitter cold — with starlight bright,
Quite late – do you remember?

And other times — one night in May,
A year ago — recall it?
When you said no – oh awful day!
It seemed to blot out every ray
Of hope – and life right with it.

The picture also calls to mind
My dreams – with all their fervor,
But it's no dream – in you I find
The essence of all womankind —
You hold my heart forever.

La Goulette, Tunis
June, 1943

Where Roses Bloomed

The garden where the roses bloomed last spring
Was full of fragrance — and the birds did sing.
Do you believe we once met there to vow
We'd be forever true — or was it then as now
A pleasant dream?

The lilacs' perfume filled the air above,
And made the' unwary couple think of love.
Did rustling breaths of wind in trees foretell
Of raptures, ecstasies for us — or is it still
A wishful dream?

The violets, lilacs, roses cannot say
If I'll come back again to you some day —
To stroll once more down paths I can't forget.
If I return, will you be there – or is it yet
A hopeless dream?

La Goulette, Tunis
July 1943

Look Forward

The days in swift succession pass on
Into the unreachable past;
That happens now is but a fragment
Of tomorrow's yesterday.
One cannot hold to the present,
For it is gone in a twinkling —
And becomes but a memory.

Think then, on the future —
For there is where you must live.
Plan, and dream, and build for days
As yet unborn —
And if the mighty palaces
Do not materialize — think not
Your plans are in vain —
Just start to build all over again.

La Goulette, Tunis
July 943

196

A Midsummer Valentine

The date for Valentines is past—- I know,
But to wait six months or so
To say again – "I love you, dear" —
Is much too long, I fear.

Therefore, this little card I send — to you,
To say what you already knew;
For even though we're miles apart,
You're always in my heart.

La Goulette, Tunis
July, 1943

Apology

I'm hopeless as a poet,
As you no doubt can see —
But I don't seem to know it,
It doesn't bother me.

I write a bunch of verses,
And think I'm doing great,
They do not fill my purses,
Nor set me up in state.

And yet I keep on writing,
Though sometimes quite in vain;
For I enjoy my scribbling,
Although I sound insane.

La Goulette, Tunis
July 1943

Thank you dear reader, for reading this book, produced jointly by Arnleif and Marie Jensen.